TEIGNMOUTH AT WAR 2

Memories of 1939 to 1945
from
The People of Teignmouth

Written & Published by Viv Wilson

First published November 2002

© Viv Wilson 2002

Designed and Printed by Exeprint, Exeter
Email : sales@exeprint.co.uk

Proof Reader: Dick Petherick of Teignmouth 01626 775539

ACKNOWLEDGEMENTS

Once again, the people of Teignmouth and District opened their doors and hearts to contribute all the material and photographs in this, the second volume of wartime memories. I am deeply honoured by the generosity, frankness of nature and warm-heartedness bestowed upon me during my researches.

Special Thanks

Teignmouth & Shaldon Museum
Syd Hook
Jim & Eileen Stowers
Pat Penwill
Pauline Rossi
Peter Ridler
Joan Mundy
Doris Pidgeon

Author's Note

Information contained in this volume was recorded in good faith and every endeavour was made to be accurate. If, however, any reader wishes to debate a point, the author will be pleased to hear from them. She hopes that it will broaden the knowledge and understanding of the wartime era in a local setting, bringing pride to the families recorded for posterity and pleasure to all its readers.

ISBN 0-9539523-1-2

Written & Published by Viv Wilson

ARP & Fire Service Personnel testing gas masks in Teignmouth Town Hall

EXTRACTS FROM TEIGNMOUTH POST 12TH JULY 1940

Hour of Destiny

In the lurid light of this titanic struggle some facts are revealed in vivid outline. We are much surer than we were. We know our enemy. We have seen his ruthlessness. We have watched his methods. His dictated terms to France and his policy of harsh oppression wherever his power extends leave us no illusions as to our fate if Hitler were to win. We know our friends. If some allies have failed us, others are rallying ever more strongly to our side, with the sturdy men of the Dominions and the growing sympathy and practical aid of the great American nations. We know ourselves. We can be justly proud not only of the fighting forces but the courage and steadfastness of one whole people. The Defence Forces have proved their mettle. Industry is putting up a magnificent show. Air raids fail to shake our nerves. We know our cause. We live in an hour of destiny. On our faithfulness depends the future of liberty and justice, freedom of thought and worship-all that is meant by Christian civilization. Service in so great a cause calls forth greatness. Britain is writing one of the noblest pages in her long story.

Teignmouth Town Hall, Brunswick St 1930s

EXTRACTS FROM TEIGNMOUTH POST 12TH JULY 1940

Chairman of Urban District Council at Bitton House - Air Raid Shelters

Four official shelters to accommodate 50 persons each are being constructed. In addition, the basement of the Riviera Cinema (for 60) and the lavatories at the rear of the Royal Hotel (for 50) are also designated as official shelters. Teignmouth will provide a little in excess of the maximum figure stated by the Government of 3 per cent of the town's normal resident population.

The Report Centre of the Air Raid Precaution - ARP

A protected basement is to be established in the lower floor of Bitton House. It will be manned day and night by teams of volunteers in shifts of six people. Brig J. Morrison appeals to the public for floor coverings, couches, camp beds, and armchairs to enable the men and women who undertake this important work to do so in reasonable comfort.

The Board of Education

New instructions issued on precautions to be taken by schools during air raids: If bombs drop without warning near schools, children should take up the safest position in the building and lie on the floor, away from windows. On no account must they leave the building to enter the school or domestic shelters.

Several original 'Kernal's Pals'

An Auxiliary Unit of Home Guard 203 was part of a so-called Secret Army hurriedly set up by Col Colin McVean Gubbins in 1940. In Devon, 140 civilians were embraced into this British Resistance group. Formed into teams of 6 or 7 men, they would be in the front line in the event of invasion and were the first to be issued with Tommy guns, plastic explosive, sticky bombs and cyanide pills. Had Hitler's troops invaded, the group was to organize attacks from the underground hide-outs, supply stores and arms dumps they had created up to 20 feet below the surface. The Stand Down came in 1944 but because their existence was still confidential information, they received no public recognition.

L-R Back   **Ernie Gover : Sgt Cecil Gilpin : Commander AW Eardley : Cpl Arthur Carpenter : Sid Thorpe**
Front   **Cecil Hatherly : Bill Leaman : Reggie Penhaligon : ?**

12TH BATTALION DEVONSHIRE REGIMENT
6TH AIRBORNE DIVISION

The British Army had no airborne formations at the onset of war but a capability was built up by 1942. The new force was granted the right to wear the famous dark red beret and the insignia of the flying horse, Pegasus. Transportation would be by un-armed monoplane Horsa gliders constructed of spruce, covered in fabric. The main parts were made in different areas of the country. Boulton Paul Company constructed the nose sections at Melton Mowbray after their Norwich base was bombed out and burnt down in 1940. The gliders' 29-metre wingspan and fuselage length of 26 metres had a tricycle undercarriage. A plexiglass canopy provided good visibility for the two pilots. The RAF did the final assembly work and towed them on Y-shaped wires with Albemarles, Halifaxes or Sterlings. A telephone cable enabled the pilots of both craft to communicate as they flew in tandem. Gliders could carry 28 fully equipped troops, or two jeeps, or a 75mm howitzer or a 6 pdr anti-tank gun – even a light truck. Pilots were trained to land slowly to preserve the nose from where it was unloaded. Troops were strapped into floor seats and linked arms and raised their feet during landings. If a rapid exit was required, they hacked straight out through the fuselage.

Horsa Glider at Melton Mowbray Airfield 1945

Matthew "Jock" Campbell collected this photograph when he was Deputy Chief Inspector of Boulton Paul in 1942, over-seeing preparation work on the gliders' nose parts. Jock and his family moved to Teignmouth in the 1970s and became involved in the local theatrical scene.

12TH BATTALION DEVONSHIRE REGIMENT
6TH AIRBORNE DIVISION

Pegasus Bridge, Normandy 5th June 1944

Early in 1944, various sections of 6th Airborne Division were stationed at Salisbury Plain training under Major General Richard Gale. Bad weather caused D-Day to be postponed for 24 hours and on the final day glider troops and parachutists ate their last meal and posted letters home. Seaborne troops were already on the way to Normandy. The airborne men blackened their faces with charcoal and crossed the airfields, heavily loaded down with grenades, rifles and ammunition. At four minutes past 11pm on 5th June, the first of six Halifax bombers connected to a silent-flying glider took off. Five others followed at intervals of one minute. At midnight they slipped past anti-aircraft defences on the French coast, the gliders cast off at 2000 feet. Rapid landings were followed by the start of the first British assault at Normandy.

The Rhine Crossing 24th March 1945

The Battle for the Rhine was the biggest military operation since D-Day. British, American and Canadian troops were to cross the Rhine under the command of Field Marshal Montgomery. The ground force was joined by an armada of airborne troops transported by 3000 aircraft from almost thirty bases in Britain and on the Continent. The Devon's had trained specifically for the capture of Hammenkelin and seized the enemy communications centre within an hour of landing. The troops lived rough on the ground and survived on iron rations of biscuits and boxes of cheese. The speed and weight of the Allied onslaught broke morale and the enemy surrendered at the rate of 10-12,000 each day. One great city after another fell to the victorious Allies leading to the final and unconditional surrender signed on 9th May 1945.

Cpl Robert Barge 6th Airborne Division

Born in Parson St in 1916, Bob married local girl Win Rose in 1942 with the worst part of the war still ahead. On the dawn of D-Day, he was involved in the capture of Pegasus Bridge at Normandy. He was also amongst those who flew from three airfields on 24th March 1945 for the Battle of the Rhine. Eleven days later, Bob and his Londoner pal Sid Dillon were wounded and Bob convalesced for six months in a Belgian Hospital. Every year, on 6th June, survivors make a pilgrimage to Normandy. One of the photographs displayed at the British Airborne Museum, built near Pegasus Bridge in 1973 shows Bob and Sid, two of the brave Airborne men who fought their way through a very dangerous episode. Bob never shared those experiences with his wife and children, Linda and David, in whom he delighted. He returned to the grocery trade, created a large and productive garden and later worked at Centrax. The author is proud to have known this quiet, blue-eyed, unassuming man for a short while before his death in 1997.

Pte Ken Hookway 6th Airborne Division

Born in Bickford Lane in 1925, Ken was training as a compositor with Brunswick Press when the Fire Station adjacent was bombed in August 1942. A few months before his 18th birthday, he was drafted into the 12th Devonshire Regiment and joined more than one thousand men stationed at Bulford camp. Initially trained as a rifleman, Ken had practice flights for D-Day in Horsa gliders over Salisbury Plain. Dakotas towed them up to practice flying and landing. "It was an enjoyable experience and I wasn't scared although I was one of the youngest...the

men were happy all together." He was bitterly disappointed that there were not enough gliders for all the Airborne troops so on the evening of the D-Day landings, his company went to Benfleet in Essex to board landing craft and cross by sea. Fighting was already underway by the time they arrived. Ken, armed with a bren gun, located his division and fought alongside his best friend from Paignton who was killed. It was expected that British ground forces would relieve them but the company stayed out there for three months and got involved with intermittent fighting. Moving around different areas, they occupied chateaux, farmhouses and other empty buildings. The 12th Devon's were involved in taking Honfleur. Testament to the heavy casualties can be witnessed by 2500 graves at Ranville's Airborne Cemetery in Normandy. Ken suffered no injuries and learned to accept good times

with the bad. As with countless others, his youth was requisitioned by king and country. His memories remain firmly in place. "You never forget what you've been through," says Ken who survived his local comrades of the 6th Airborne and lives quietly in the town.

LC Robert Rawlings 6th Airborne Division

Robert, born 1920 in Newton Abbot married Mary Glover of Teignmouth. His wartime scrapbook includes a faded cutting of Reuter's Correspondent report of the British Paratroops.

"The first British tank to reach the sky troops who were dropped beyond the Rhine came round a

12TH BATTALION DEVONSHIRE REGIMENT
6TH AIRBORNE DIVISION

bend in the road today under the protection of our anti-tank guns after a dash of nine miles through woods held by Germans. Our paratroopers cheered this first muddy and battle-worn crusader. The great airborne blow which demoralized the Germans by a sudden and violent descent in their rear is all over now-but the price was not light. The fields of the Reich where we landed are littered with smashed and burned-out gliders. Among them are multi-coloured parachutes which looked like great gay flowers. A number of our men landed in the trees and were killed as they hung in their parachutes. We must have looked a fearsome crowd with our blackened faces, jumping smocks and camouflaged helmets. We had to get clear of the landing zone to avoid being pinned down by German fire, as the gliders were following ready to come in when opposition had been eliminated. Soon the sky was filled with the roar of hundreds of planes over a small area at once, sweeping through heavy flak. By then the Germans had recovered from the surprise of the first landings and threw everything they had, including 88mm shells at the paratroops planes, gliders and the Stirlings and Halifaxes towing them. The gliders suffered the most casualties mainly from incendiary flak shells which sent numbers of them down like flying torches. We had a high proportion of crashes, mostly due to ground fog which confused the pilots. They crashed into trees and houses and turned somersaults in the fields. All around, great bursts of flame shot out from the wreckage. The hunting horn of the paratroops commanders sounded the tally-ho to rally the units. German flak guns barked incessantly as streams of aircraft including supply planes roared above our heads less than 50 feet up and some Dakotas screamed over with flames streaming from them. There was little sleep for us in our slit trench. At daylight today, air battles began as the Luftwaffe tried to disrupt our supplies and reinforcements but they were outnumbered ten to one and one after another fell in flames close to us.

Within ten minutes of crash-landing their glider into a farmyard east of the Rhine, nine Devon's captured twice as many prisoners as there were British troops who poured out of the glider. Sgt Hodge of Exmouth told a military observer "We were hit by flak but crashed uninjured…we leapt out of the glider with wild yells and dashed straight for the double doors to shoot up any enemy who felt like giving the Airborne a scrap. As we went in the front door, Germans were streaming out at the back and coming pell-mell up the cellar steps to get away from the Red Devils as the prisoners now call the Airborne men. They threw their weapons at our feet and surrendered."

The Devon's, in a lightening advance to within 100 miles of Berlin, captured village after village and a number of small defended towns. Bob returned to the building trade. He trained Cadets at Totnes Drill Hall in the 70s where he was Caretaker and died in 1984.

12TH BATTALION DEVONSHIRE REGIMENT
6TH AIRBORNE DIVISION

The Airborne Forces' Prayer

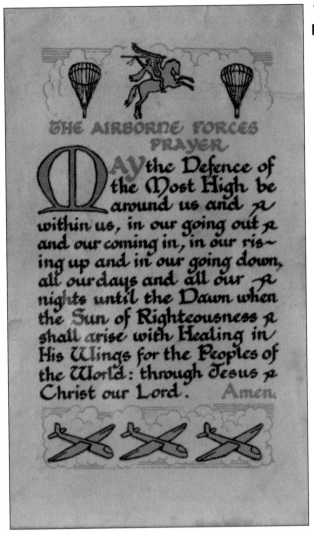

THE AIRBORNE FORCES PRAYER

MAY the Defence of the Most High be around us and within us, in our going out and our coming in, in our rising up and in our going down, all our days and all our nights until the Dawn when the Sun of Righteousness shall arise with Healing in His Wings for the Peoples of the World: through Jesus Christ our Lord. Amen.

Pte Ernest Robins 6th Airborne Division

Ernest was born in Saxe St in 1914. He was a very placid man and as a trainee barber, shaved male patients at the hospital. Later, he trained in Ladies hairdressing and was just getting going when the Call Up came. Ern, aged 28, turned to his mother and said, "Enjoy yourself...it's later than you think". He was based first at Okehampton Army Camp and then at

12TH BATTALION DEVONSHIRE REGIMENT
6TH AIRBORNE DIVISION

Plymouth. Little is known of Ern's war but as part of the 6th Airborne he was in the Normandy landings and the Rhine Crossing. In 1948, he became suddenly ill at the family home above his hairdressing shop at the bottom of Bitton Park Rd. He was rushed to hospital in Exeter with pernicious anaemia – now called leukaemia. Ern died tragically early at the age of 34 but is remembered with deep affection by his sister Doris and sister-in-law, Pat.

Pte Harold Webber 6th Airborne Division

Harold, serving with the 6th Airborne, was landed at a beach near Honfleur, Normandy on 7th June 1944 – D-Day + 1. Together with the driver of a special vehicle shipped over for the purpose, his responsibility was to locate and transport water supplies to his unit. Airborne and Seaborne troops linked up to drive the enemy back from the beaches and fierce fighting for Caen extended across several days. The Germans had hastily thrown up anti-tank ditches and strong defences to try to stem the Allied advance. The 6th Airborne successfully held the Orne estuary and ground forces were supported by a heavy bombardment from Allied battleships on 13th June. The unit dug themselves into foxholes around an area of orchards, becoming accustomed to sleeping under saturated blankets. After three months they returned to Bulford Camp but in December, his Division was rushed out to Ardennes, Belgium where several divisions had been thrown into the offensive after the enemy drove a 25-mile wedge into American lines. The weather was bitter and at one point their vehicle slid off the road, Harold losing all his belongings. Christmas dinner of corned beef was served to the unit as they took shelter in a barn. The Rhine itself provided

a useful water supply but Harold sometimes had to dip into private wells, an action not readily accepted by locals. On one of the sorties to find a supply, he was immediately concerned they were heading the wrong way when he noticed the lack of communication lines beside the road. Suddenly, their vehicle hit a landmine. It exploded beneath Harold and he was pulled out backwards from beneath the burning vehicle. His face was burned and his left eye needed stitches but in a letter home written from a Brussels hospital on 22nd April 1945, he reassured his wife Ethel that he was doing well. He was brought back to a Liverpool Hospital, missing VE Day celebrations at home. As with so many Servicemen, Harold kept his war experiences to himself but his widow Ethel remembers that he was just glad to be back home safe in Teignmouth.

CIVIL DEFENCE

No. 5

PUBLIC INFORMATION LEAFLET

READ THIS CAREFULLY AND KEEP IT FOR
REFERENCE

FIRE PRECAUTIONS
IN
WAR TIME

ISSUED FROM
THE LORD PRIVY SEAL'S OFFICE
AUGUST 1939

British Waterworks Association
(INCORPORATED)

President :
~~rman~~ C. W. BEARDSLEY, J.P.,
Shelfield Corporation.

Secretary :
~~ARD~~ W. F. MILLIS, B.Sc.(Econ.),
Barrister-at-Law.

Tel. No. : WHitehall 0082

GRAND BUILDINGS
TRAFALGAR SQUARE
LONDON, W.C.2

March, 1941

HINTS TO HOUSEHOLDERS ON WATER PURIFICATION.

The British Waterworks Association has prepared instructions as to how water should be treated if, as a result of air raids, it became necessary to use impure or doubtful water.

Water Undertakers will, of course, take all possible precautions to enable a constant supply of pure water to be maintained, but after an air raid this may be temporarily impracticable and it is, therefore, necessary for every citizen to know how to treat impure water so that it would be safe for drinking, the preparation of food, and for washing utensils which are to be used for food or drink.

Read the instructions very carefully; see that you understand them; and save the pamphlet for future reference in case an emergency should arise.

C. W. BEARDSLEY,
President.

LEONARD W. F. MILLIS,
Secretary.

A. EMERGENCY SUPPLY OF DRINKING WATER.

A supply of pure drinking water sufficient to tide over a short emergency of, say, two or three days should be kept ready for use if the supply to your premises is cut off by enemy action. The water is best stored in clean stoppered bottles kept in a cool dark place. It is not necessary to use this water for making tea as boiling will rid any water of disease germs.

[P.T.O.

Fred Avery

I was a choirboy in St Michael's Church on 3rd September 1939 when Douglas Chapple came to tell Rev Wyatt that war was declared. Some people began to cry quietly. I was 13 and World War 1 was an unknown horror but older people knew only too well what might lie ahead. The first bomb attack in July 1940 occurred during a church service. There was a loud roar and two sharp bangs. It didn't seem right to hear a thing like that in a church. I sat in the cockpit of a shot-down ME 109 displayed near the lighthouse. It was an eerie feeling that a German pilot had sat there, a man trained to kill me. I worked at Morgan Giles shipyard and became an apprentice joiner. It was excellent training as the quality of the work was superb. RN officers due for command of an MTB hoped it coincided with delivery of a Morgan Giles built craft. They were exciting boats, particularly when bouncing along at 40 knots. Looking aft during high-speed turns, the whole boat seemed to slightly twist and it was reassuring to know that it was really well built!

In addition to day work, staff did Fire Watch duties with teams of six taking turns to stay in the yard all night. It was a strange, spooky place in the dark, the tide slapping the steel doors on the slipway and stray rats running about. I was on duty the night of 18th May 1943 when the only incendiary bomb attack occurred across the river in Bitton Park. We were mighty glad the yard wasn't hit - how we would have fought any fire in all that clutter I can't imagine. I was a cadet in ATC 60 Sqdn and on Sundays walked up to Haldon Aerodrome to help by running messages, or picking up drogues dropped by Skua aircraft and counting bullet holes scored by trainee pilots. We hoped for a flight in a Fulmar but were just a few "odd-bods" doing a lot of running around. Much to our annoyance, all flights were taken up by cadets from Torquay or Newton Abbot who came in squads, complete with an officer to look after their interests. Ernest Rose didn't get a flight until a few days before joining the RAF and from then on it was a different story for him. (See page 73 Teignmouth at War 1)

Going to the pictures was a great escape. The Carlton and Riviera Cinemas were well patronized, particularly by all the service people. Shows were continuous, and this usually meant a queue outside. As seats became available, we shuffled forward until we got in and often found that the film was almost finished so we knew that "the butler did it" right away! It ruined the story when the end came round again.

Forte's Milk Bar in the Triangle was a favourite place after the pictures and on ATC parade nights. Louis and his brother and their sister Donna created a pleasant spot for coffee and chat. They suffered some harassment when Italy came into the war but there was very little trouble around the town. Saturday night dances at the London Hotel were a big attraction for locals and military. It was always crowded and had a touch of glamour to round off the working week. Going home in the Blackout, we never felt at risk of being set-upon by louts – more so from slipping off the kerb, walking into a lamp post or even another pedestrian. The glow of a cigarette was a great help and we hoped it didn't help enemy pilots target us. Air attacks at night were usually by a single aircraft and some German bombers misread the geography of the

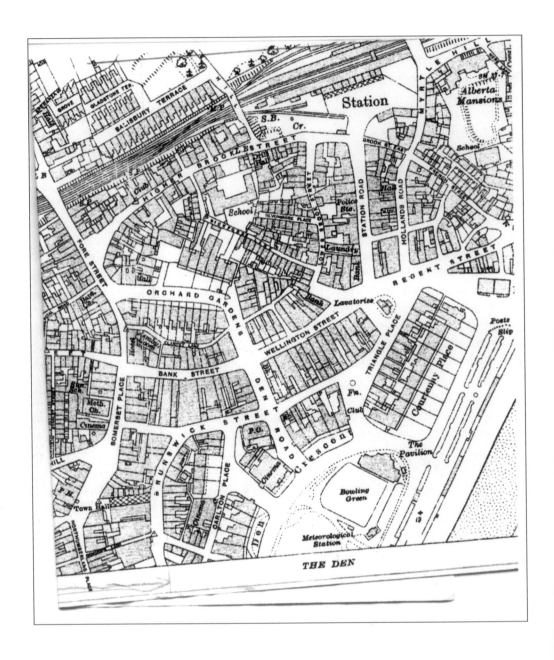

14

area and lost their way. One, returning to base via South Wales crossed the Bristol Channel, saw the coast ahead and thinking it was France, lowered his undercarriage and made a good landing at an airfield. Unfortunately for him, it was North Devon and the plane was captured intact and sent to Farnborough for evaluation. The Blackout, radio silence and unsophisticated instruments caused many such mistakes of location.

Deadly fighters FW 190s carried out quick, sharp daylight raids all along the coast from Kent to Devon. I believe Teignmouth was targeted not particularly for any military or industrial reasons but because it was a readily identified landfall. Coming in fast and low, a pilot didn't have much time to pick his target. He would have seen a line of fairly high red cliffs all the way from Torquay to Dawlish, broken only by the town and river beyond: a row of prominent buildings lining the frontage from Eastcliff to the Point: the rest of the town rising behind and a wide, easily seen river beyond. It was an easy aiming point and, having made an attack, the river was a good place to turn for a final shoot-up before heading back out to sea. This paragraph will take longer to read than the duration of a "tip and run" raid. It is amazing that attacks were never made on the most vulnerable section of railway line between Eastcliff and Dawlish. Defended only by a few machine gun posts and beach barriers, frontal attacks by low flying aircraft could have breached the sea wall or brought down material from the cliffs. Bearing in mind German expertise in Storm Trooper and airborne warfare as used in Europe, Commando-type raids would have caused havoc. I often wonder how the older people coped with life during those sad and worrying days with rationing and lack of everyday things as well as the safety of family members away in the forces. I simply cannot imagine how I would feel if those conditions were imposed on me today.

**Pilot's eye
view 1930s**

BANGS & LAKEMAN FAMILY

Pte Walter Bangs Devonshire Regiment

Walter, a Londoner, married local girl May Lakeman in the 1920s and their children were Ron, Pauline and June. He worked as a Decorator from their home in Dagmar St, Shaldon and was in middle age when he was called up first to the Devonshire Regiment, transferring later to the Manchester Regiment. Whilst he was guarding Italian Prisoners of War in Scotland, one of them made an exquisite cotton frame of red, white and blue around a little photo of Pauline that Walter carried with him.

Ron Bangs

Shaldon's Home Guard in 1943 with mother and sisters Pauline (R) and June

Ron went to work for the Railway at the age of 16. It was a reserved occupation and Ron was involved in signal maintenance, erecting telegraph poles and wires alongside the tracks across mid-Devon. In the same year he became a "Runner" in Shaldon's Home Guard, dashing between the village and the top of Commons Lane with messages. Ron worked on the railway for 43 years and retired to Teignmouth.

William Henry Lakeman 1943
Grandfather to the Bangs children, William was one of the oldest in Shaldon's Home Guard. Being a semi-invalid did not stop him playing his part in defending the village by manning the HG telephone.

Albert Lakeman
Brother to May, Albert served in the Queen's Royal Regiment

CIVIL DEFENCE

YOUR GAS MASK

How to keep it
and How to Use it

—

MASKING YOUR WINDOWS

—

PUBLIC INFORMATION
LEAFLET   NO. 2

Read   this   and
keep   it   carefully.
You may need it.

Issued from the Lord Privy Seal's Office July, 193

Alternatively, thick curtains of suitable material will serve, if they really cover the window frames with a bit to spare all round.

The simplest way of testing material, whether for blinds or curtains, is to hold up a piece against an electric bulb. If no light shows through, or only scattered pin holes of light are seen, then the material will do. If a patch of light shows through, it is no use.

Possibly you have blinds already fitted to your windows. If the material is not sufficiently opaque, you can treat it with Oil Bound Water Paint or Distemper of some dark colour. The following mixture can be applied with a brush :—

1 lb. of concentrated size, 3 lb. lamp black in powder form, ½ gill of gold size. The size and lamp black should be thoroughly mixed and 2½ gallons of boiling water added. This quantity will cover about 80 square yards of material.

If your blinds do not fit very closely, you could paint the edges of the window panes all round with dark paint. It will, of course, help if you also shade your lights so as to prevent any light falling directly on the window.

Most Important—do not forget your skylight if you have one, or glazed doors or even fanlights. You may find it simplest to make these permanently obscure by applying sufficient coats of some dark distemper or paint, or pasting them over with thick brown paper.

There is another thing to remember—Make sure that no light shows when your front door or back door is open. In some cases it may be possible to fix a curtain in the hall or passage to form a " light lock," but if this cannot be done, the light must be turned off before the door is opened.

Some people perhaps will only use one or two rooms at night in war time. This, of course, would simplify matters considerably, as the precautions indicated would only have to be taken for those particular rooms. But you would have to take care not to show by mistake any light in a room where the windows were not screened, and also to see that light did not reach the window of an unoccupied room through some open door.

Do not leave things until the last, but get together the materials which you think you would need. If you wait, you might find that you had difficulty in getting what you wanted. Besides, your help is wanted in making effective the " black-outs " for the A.R.P. exercises which are being arranged to try out our defences from time to time.

After all, it is only common sense to make our preparations in advance to meet a possible emergency.

[63-4154]

Win Barge nee Rose

The Rose family lost all their possessions when their home in Bitton St was bombed out on 2nd July 1942. Six months later, Win married Bob Barge with whom she had worked at Burton's grocery store, opposite the London Hotel in Bank St. Bob was serving with the 6th Airborne Division. The family moved to Abingdon after Win's father William was given a job of national importance, driving Queen Mary lorries, transporting aircraft components. Win became a welder of aircraft parts in the former MG car factory.

Remnants of camouflaged gun location (L) beside Ness Drive 1940s

LAFO Hubert Bartlett (L) 825 Naval Air Sqd

Bomb Disposal - outskirts of Hong Kong 1945

Born in Albion St, Shaldon in 1924, Bert became an apprentice plumber to JS Scown. He joined the Royal Navy and transferred to the Fleet Air Arm to train in aircraft armoury. Soon after volunteering for a sea-going draft, Bert was off aboard HMS Vindex (825 RNAS) on Atlantic patrols. The ship later joined convoys to Russia and helped smash an all-out attack by U-boats to stop arms and war stores getting through the icy seas of the Arctic Circle. The single engine Swordfish aircraft carried four rockets on each wing and a depth charge in the centre. Bert served next on HMS Campania and after the squadron was disbanded, he was issued with khaki uniform and sent out to Australia on Mobile Operational Naval Air Bases. At Kai-Tek near Hong Kong he was guarding Japanese POWs on working parties. In the Bomb Disposal Unit, he dealt with nine bombs including one of 500 pounds at Shaukiwan. It took 7 hours to immunize and as a leading hand, Bert had to stay with the officer until the fuse was removed on all occasions. Bert joined hundreds gathered for the Christmas Day service in Hong Kong Cathedral and got into conversation with an Army Pay Corps Sergeant standing beside him. He was amazed to discover that the wife of this man, whom he had never seen before, was the tenant of a house owned and occupied by Bert's parents in Bristol. On 1st April 1946 he boarded a troop ship with 5000 others and arrived on

British soil one month later. He returned to Mr Scown under the government's interrupted apprenticeship scheme. He married Doreen later that year and worked as a plumber with Wilkins of Torquay, Contractors building Teignmouth's post war hospital. The Bartletts enjoy retirement, maintaining a large and productive garden.

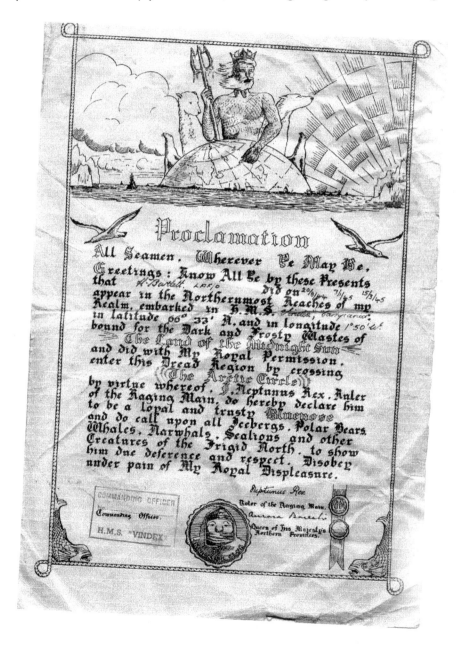

Proclamation by CO of HMS Vindex

James William Belton Shipwright

Jim was born in Teignmouth in 1923. As a shipwright he repaired and serviced Landing Craft Assault vessels. LCAs were about 30 feet in length and carried 30 men. He made 37 trips on the Normandy Landings aboard Queen Beatrice, a troop landing ship modified on the Clyde. Jim resumed his career as a shipwright at Morgan Giles and after the yard closed in 1968, he built fine boats on his own account. Years later he was invited to go to Normandy for D-Day Remembrance and said, "No thanks – I went there once and it was bloody awful!" Jim died in 2001.

British Legion HQ Den Crescent founded in 1926

BLADON FAMILY

Frederick William Bladon

Chief Fire Officer ARP preparing for fire or incendiary bombs at Lugano, Courtenay Terrace

Frederick served in World War One with the Royal Army Medical Corps. Being a Conscientious Objector, he carried no weapons. In World War Two he was Chief Fire Officer for Teignmouth's Air Raid Precautions and rejected the annual honorarium of £500, believing that with all three sons in the services, the money would serve a better purpose in helping to defend the country. FWB was Chairman of Teignmouth Urban District Council 1947-48.

Ethel May Bladon SRN

Staff and patients at Lugano during Coronation Celebrations 1937

Ethel was Matron of Hammersmith Hospital before moving to Teignmouth to run Lugano as a Convalescent Home in 1917. She also became deeply involved in assisting with the health of the local community. Ethel served the church of Our Lady & St Patrick faithfully and donated a stained glass window of St. Joseph near the altar.

BLADON FAMILY

Flight Sergeant Frederick Ramsay Bladon

Before Commission in 1941

Frederick, born in 1917 was 2 months old when he was brought to live at Lugano. His first flight in a Tiger Moth from Haldon Aerodrome in 1933 cost five shillings. The pilot was William Parkhouse who put Teignmouth on the air map. The following year he joined the RAF at Cranwell as a Boy Wireless Operator and the name of "Boy" stuck forever after. He completed a tour of duty lasting 3 years in Singapore and returned to England early in 1939. As part of the British Expeditionary Forces facing annihilation after being cut off in France in May 1940, Boy's unit tried to reach Dunkirk but ran out of fuel. It took them four days to make their way from St Nazaire to Brest where they got a passage home on a destroyer. Boy trained as a pilot and flying instructor and was commissioned as a Flight Lieutenant in 1941. He carried out 19 bombing operations in Wellingtons, Halifaxes and Sterlings. During a raid over Hamburg, the fragility of existence came home to him for the first time when the plane directly in front of him was hit. In a split second, a pall of thick black smoke laden with debris enveloped the aircraft and it was oblivion for the crew. "I realized that one minute you're there and the next you're gone. It was frightening to be up there. I still remember my feet vibrating on the rudder bar. Anyone who says he wasn't scared is a liar. People may think you're brave, but it's not bravery, it's training. The good thing about the RAF was the way they treated the families of those killed in action. They sorted out their belongings and raised what money they could. The CO always wrote a good letter to them."

Boy transported troops to India until VJ Day then returned to peaceful Teignmouth. He married and started up a 24-hour taxi business in Waterloo St. In 2002, he continues to revel in the daily delights of the river beach.

BLADON FAMILY

Sgt Geoffrey P.R. Bladon 115 Squadron

Geoff, born 1919, volunteered for the RAF in 1936 and became a Sergeant in 115 Squadron. He was a very brave man and helped rescue a colleague trapped by a bomb that had rolled off an aircraft during loading. In his years of service from August '37 to September '46, he had only 91 days leave. As a Rear Gunner flying daytime raids in Sterlings and Wellington bombers, Geoff gained several medals: Air Crew Europe, Africa Star and clasp, Italy Star, M.I.D, Atlantic Star and clasp, War Medal, King's Commendation and oak leaf attachments. Geoff's son Paul now cherishes his father's medals and RAF jacket.

By the KING'S ORDER

The name of Sergeant G.P.R. Bladon Royal Air Force was published in the London Gazette on 17 September 1943 as mentioned in a Despatch for distinguished service. I am charged to record His Majesty's high appreciation.

Archibald Sinclair   **Secretary of State for Air**

CPO Arthur Leonard Bladon

Arthur, born 1921 signed on for 22 years service with the Royal Navy in 1939. He became a Chief Petty Officer and served on the British Battleship Warspite, a ship with which he shared an affinity. In March 1941 she was en route to Greece with other ships in the Mediterranean fleet when she was engaged in the Battle of Matapan. A few weeks later the ship's side was laid open by an enemy bomb and several of Arthur's group were killed by the blast. The explosion blew Arthur through a doorway and hole in the adjoining bulkhead and he was left badly injured, peppered with shrapnel. Warspite limped off for repair but in 1947 ended her life as a wreck off Cornwall, close to her Devonport birthplace.

Arthur was a very lucky man, avoiding certain death

at least three times. He was drafted to HMS Hood but swapped - the ship went down. In November 1941, whilst serving on Barham he was due for shore leave but his replacement did not arrive until the ship was about to put to sea. At the last minute, Arthur was given permission to go ashore. It was to be that ship's last voyage. Three torpedoes from a German submarine hit Barham's ammunition magazine. It exploded and 862 crew members were lost. Arthur saw service in all theatres of war, gaining the Atlantic Star, Pacific Star, African Star and Burma Star clasp. He was transferred to Admiralty staff and ended up at Portsmouth from where he was demobbed in 1945 on a naval disability pension. A piece of shrapnel that got lodged in his back on Warspite led him to suffer for the remainder of his life. He became an hotelier at the former family home Lugano (now Redcliffs) married Marjorie and raised Geoff and Gregory. Following his father's footsteps he served on Teignmouth Urban District Council and was its Chairman from 1965-69. He bought Shaldon's Dunmore Hotel, demolished in 1974 and replaced by apartments but he retained its garden and built a home from where he could overlook the town he loved. He was Chairman of Teignbridge District Council 1980-82 and became a Devon County Councillor, achieving a tremendous amount during his time in local politics. After Arthur's death in 1990, Bladon Close in Newton Abbot was named in his memory.

Lt Gordon Bond

I was born in Newton Abbot and my family moved to Teignmouth in 1929 when Grandfather Vinnicombe took over the Wine & Spirits business in Northumberland Place and bonded warehouses on the quay. I attended Teignmouth Grammar School and played in its football and cricket teams. I joined the Army early in 1940 and was placed in the Royal Signals. We were based at a house outside Crediton where each morning I was out at 5am with 20 chaps trying to wash and shave at the same time using a solitary cold tap. I was supposed to be trained to use a radio but we were in a terrible state because there weren't any radios. We drove around in a Humber pick-up as if we were running a group of stations when all we had were empty boxes that looked like radios. We were moved to up to Battle in Sussex and practised defending Hastings beach with pitchforks because there were no guns. The lack of weapons shook me more than anything. Just before the war started I had been to Southampton to see the Queen Mary, beautifully built by our shipbuilders yet here we were, totally unprepared to go to war, with no guns and no radios. I learned Morse code and eventually we acquired radios from the USA. I became a commissioned officer and had nine months training at Catterick before transferring to Scotland to form the new 78th Infantry division. We sailed on a ship called Sobieski, landing 8th November 1942. It was a very nasty war in North Africa. We took Algiers first then Tunis, held for a long time by the Germans. I sent home a copy of the first Tunis Telegraph to be printed after we took it in '43 and it was re-printed on the front page of the Teignmouth Post on 25th June 1943. I was allocated a 500cc motorbike that had been on the deck of the ship and manhandled down into a dinghy during the journey. I rode it down through olive groves to rendezvous with a unit. Little did I know that there was a large sand heap in front of the GoC, ran right into it, did a somersault and landed at his feet! He didn't take kindly to it and neither did I! Whilst home on leave I experienced a couple of hit and run raids and thought I'd rather be back in the army where there was less damage!

Freda Bond (L) and friends in front of South View, overlooking Den in 1944. Note brick shelter, top of Brunswick St (R)

Leading Seaman William Patrick Boyne

Born in Teignmouth 1896, William served in World War One. In 1940 he volunteered for RN River Patrol that used two former pleasure boats, re-named HMS Hindustan and HMS Valiant, both moored off Ivy Lane. William and Sydney Briggs left for Dunkirk but were recalled after reaching the Isle of Wight. William was coxswain of Hindustan, Mr Knockles was Engineer and crew was Jack Belton, Curly Westlake, Kai Broom. (See photo on page 85 of Teignmouth at War 1) Duty was twelve hours on and twelve off. Each night at high water, they reported to the Bofor Battery at Gravel Point about halfway upriver, above the bridge. When fears of German invasion with seaplanes were high, all the boats that could be mustered were moored across the Teign estuary. Navy personnel from Plymouth assisted the River Patrol to erect tripods of scaffolding poles in the river between the gas works and Coombe Cellars. The patrol was called out if a plane came down and once they were sent out to deal with a mine that had surfaced after a trawler got fouled by part of an enemy plane on the seabed. Mines dropped from planes had a sinker to keep them on the bottom but this one was floating. Hindustan stood well off and fired all the ammunition of their Canadian Hotchkiss machine gun. The mine failed to explode and had to be dealt with by an MTB from Dartmouth. During a raid near the hospital, an enemy plane circled and William ordered the engineer to fire if it re-appeared. It did and they were certain that contact was made even though the plane carried on out to sea. When they went off duty at midnight, William was told to report to Captain Rees at the Royal Hotel immediately. He thought he was in trouble for firing without permission. Captain Rees addressed an officer from the Battery at Shaldon and said "Take a good look at him...he isn't very big, is he? But he was the only man to engage the enemy last night. Well done!" The officer had apparently just received a telling-off for not opening fire from Shaldon!

John Paul Boyne AB
Aboard the cruiser Emerald

I was born in 1922 in Mulberry St and volunteered on 15th July 1940. About a dozen of us left together including Fred Sealey, Amos Lockyer, Pat McCarthy, Pat Welsh and Curly Westlake. We got kitted out with a uniform at HMS Drake at Devonport and sent to Britannia at Dartmouth where we were issued with a Canadian rifle and five rounds of ammunition, ready for the expected invasion. The Navy had requisitioned a Guest House close to Dartmouth Castle. On the slope below, three torpedoes faced across the river. Mines, laid beyond the river mouth were connected to a concrete bunker and enemy ships could be blown up at the press of a button. I joined the aircraft carrier Illustrious at Birkenhead and in March '42 went out on a big convoy. Some headed off to the Mediterranean but we carried on to Capetown and Durban. We went in to Madagascar after it had been invaded then up to Mombasa and did patrols over to Colombo. After leaving Illustrious at Durban, I joined a troop ship heading for Alexandria then on to Tobruk in May '43. I was there for 6 months before going back to Alexandria to join the depot ship, Woolwich. You got 3d a day for a good conduct badge and if you didn't take your tot of rum, you got another 3d a day. The conflict in the Med' was more or less finished by then and I joined the cruiser Emerald. We went in on Gold beach on D-Day and bombarded gun emplacements until we ran out of ammunition. We went back to Portsmouth, ammunitioned ship again and went out for a second time, landing at Sword area and helped with the breakthrough by bombarding Caen. I had to pass the ammunition over for loading into the breach of the 6-inch guns and the shells could travel up to about 12 miles. The worst time was when a bomb hit a tripod on our quarterdeck and glanced off over the side, leaving its fin behind. Later I got a draft to the Golden Hind, a depot out in Australia. At the end of a patrol, I took passage to Auckland for a courtesy visit and this was the place I liked most - the people were so friendly. After three weeks I went back to Sydney on the destroyer Whirlwind. Orders were issued for all ships to leave the harbour as news came through on the radio that the atom bomb had been dropped and the Japanese had surrendered. We went up to Hong Kong but weren't required and made our way home. I was demobbed in May 1946 and my gratuity pay for 1586 days was £73.3 shillings. I was lucky and the only time we got attacked was on D-Day. I married Alice and went back to fishing and shell fishing. We enjoy retirement overlooking the Teign.

BOYNE FAMILY

Bernard Boyne AB

I was born in 1926 and remember when the Bofors gun on the cliffs beyond the Ness hit an enemy plane and it dropped down into the water. It was always thought that it was the one that had dropped a bomb at St Marychurch killing many schoolchildren during a service. Hindustan went out to investigate. Down at Long Edge, a fisherman's mark, father saw yellow dye on the water from a parachute pack. It was used to help locate people during sea rescues. They recovered the body on the end of the parachute and brought it back to Teignmouth Police. Fighter-bombers came in at sea level and the first you heard of them was cannon fire, then bombs dropping. They carried delayed bombs so they were clear of the blast themselves. The sound was terrible. FW 190s had four cannons and two machine guns. Eight of them came in over together at one time. We saw the blaze of Plymouth burning from

Bernard Boyne on Fish Quay, one of his favourite haunts, in 2002

the bottom of Ivy Lane - it lies in line with Shaldon end of the bridge. The Germans had gone in over near Start Point and there were so many of them that all the windows in Teignmouth were shaken. We had a solid steel Anderson shelter in the garden. My brother John was in the Navy, sister Rita in the WRNS but I was still at home with my younger sisters Ivy and Marion.

I was returning from salmon fishing up the river and keeping to the Shaldon side to avoid the tripods when two Messerschmitts came overhead at Arch Brook, low enough to touch. They shot across the river and out of sight, then up around, turned and came back. Our mate in the boat behind yelled to get ashore. No doubt about it...they knew how to handle planes. They didn't fire at the houses, only in the river and sunk a wooden mooring buoy and a sand dredger. A machine gun bullet or two ricocheted into the big timbers down on the river beach and Wayne Hook dug one out. If we wanted to go fishing night times, we had to get permission from Captain Rees at the Royal Hotel. Army patrols were on the streets at night when they were worried about parachutists.

I left school at 14 and started fishing and if I hadn't had a fishing background I would have had to go in the Army when I was called up in 1944. Fred Sealey gave me a letter

HOME OFFICE

THE PROTECTION OF YOUR HOME AGAINST AIR RAIDS

READ THIS BOOK THROUGH
THEN
KEEP IT CAREFULLY

No. : F/F.......**140**......

MINISTRY OF HOME SECURITY

(FIRE GUARD INSTRUCTORS' COURSE No....157......)

I Certify that.............T.H. AGGETT..............

....attended a course at the Ministry of Home

Security School at............FALFIELD............from............30th August....., 1943,

to..........4th September.., 1943, and is **QUALIFIED** to give instruction in

methods of conducting FIRE GUARD TACTICAL TRAINING.

....
Commandant and Chief Instructor

MINISTRY OF HOME SECURITY SCHOOL,
EASTWOOD PARK,
FALFIELD, GLOS..

Date..............8th September, 1943.............

to take to Plymouth to say I had been a bona fide fisherman. The navy were cutting back so I went in the Merchant Navy on a small tanker called a Chant Boat - Chattel and Harbour Auxiliary Naval Tanker, one of about 200 flat-bottomed boats designed for going in on the beaches. At the time of the Invasion we loaded with Benzine at the old jetty at Hamble near Southampton and were at anchor near the Isle of Wight supplying fuel to MTBs and MLs, expecting to go across to France. After the Invasion we were sent to Le Havre. After Holland was re-taken by the Canadians, our 400-ton tanker was cleaned out so we could carry fresh water across the country for Dutch people because all their supply system had been destroyed. Our ship and three others collected the water from a deep-sea ship off the Hook of Holland. I did four trips on another Chant boat carrying fuel oil from Plymouth to German boats that had been captured and brought from the Channel Islands to Southampton. The navy made use of the good ships, as there was a shortage. Some of them had originally been our own ships taken by the Germans at Dunkirk, patched up and used by them. They were moored three abreast in the harbour at St Helier and St Peterport. It was my job to go aboard whilst the ships were being refuelled. The crew were just like us - civilian merchantmen, glad it was all over. They brought the ships over here then were sent home. I stayed on until 1947, met my wife and she was such a good cook I never went to sea again!

RAF 20mm Hispano anti-aircraft gun Shaldon Bridge and anti-invasion tripods in the river

Peter Bow

I was born in Hermosa Nursing Home in 1931 and remember Anderson shelters being installed even before war was declared. Morrison shelters did not appear until early 1941 and we understood we were one of the first in town to be allocated one. My parents were on the Promenade near the pier during the first raid on Sunday 7th July 1940. Father saw the plane, thought it was one of ours because of the red, white and blue roundels on the wings but soon realized the colours were reversed with the white in the centre, indicating it was a French plane. Having been a Sergeant at the Somme and Ypres, he shouted to everyone to get down when the bombs were released. I was in the kitchen at 10 Bank St at the time, scared speechless by the terrible noise of the explosions. I hid in a corner, hands clasped over my ears and Flora Peachey scolded me for being a crybaby. She was an evacuee mother of Robin, with whom I still have regular contact, 6 months younger than me and Dawn aged 3, who shared our enormous four-storey house above Creedy's Shoe Shop where father was Manager. My sister Ruth was a great friend of Beatrice James, one of the nurses killed in the raid on Teignmouth Hospital and this was my first direct contact with someone dying. Haberdasher Aske's (Hatcham) Girls' School, arrived early in 1940 for the January term but the raid of October 1941 was too close for comfort to their main hostel at Mount Everest so they moved to Barnstaple. Haberdasher Aske's (Plumstead) Boys' School was evacuated here in the summer of 1944 after London was hit by VIs. My parents offered to take an evacuee from the school, or two if it meant brothers being separated. Three unrelated boys aged from 12 to 15 were presented to her at 7pm when "no one else would take them". We already had a long-term evacuee who, as a senior boy at Teignmouth Grammar School, did fire watching at night on the school roof. I envied this job but the war finished a few months too soon for me to join this elite band. Boys could not join the school's ATC 60 Squadron until they were 14. It disbanded in favour of the Combined Cadet Force in 1947. I became a Sergeant and we had khaki uniforms but maintained the RAF connection by having blue webbing gaiters and belts. We went gliding from Exeter Airport and attended annual camps at RAF stations Cranwell and Cottesmore.

Although I was in Teignmouth for all the raids, the one that stands out was 13th August 1942. I was mounting my bicycle in the middle of George St outside our rear entrance at 5.30pm and heard the now familiar sound of gunfire and a low flying aircraft. There was no warning siren as a Focke Wulf 190 came from the direction of St Michael's Church, at rooftop height straight towards me. When it was almost directly over the Triangle, I could see the pilot and flashes from the machine guns and cannon. Then it released a bomb. Dropping my bike, I ran to the Roberts' house opposite where iron railings had been removed for the war effort. This allowed me to jump straight in behind the large left-hand gate pillar. As I crouched there, a 20mm cannon shell blew the pyramidal coping off the top of the pillar. I scurried through the Roberts' open door and reached the Morrison shelter in their front room just before the bomb hit the Town Hall. Seconds after the deafening explosions, Peter and Sheila Roberts, their mother and grandmother joined me. From the moment I first saw the plane to being in the shelter was probably less than ten seconds but in my memory now, it all happened in slow motion. The noise had partially deafened me but I could hear my mother desperately calling my name from the rubble in the street littered with debris, mostly remnants of wooden lathes from damaged buildings. Everything around us was covered in a thick grey layer of plaster dust, including my bike. Fortunately neither I - nor it - suffered any damage! Whilst re-visiting Teignmouth from South Africa in 1993, I showed my son the pillar, still minus its coping! All the windows in our house and shop were shattered along with most shop windows in the town centre. Plate glass was in short supply so repairs were done with hardboard or wood and small pieces of ordinary glass. Some of these temporary windows remained in use as late as 1950 during the difficult economic situation following the end of the war.

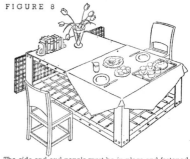

seventh stage

Put the side and end panels over the studs.
Get inside just before the last one is put into place, and fix the four hook-and-eye fastenings as shown in Figure 7.   You

FIGURE 6

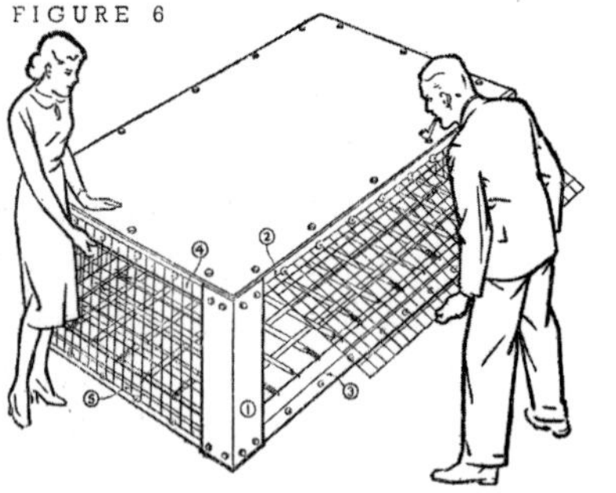

will notice in the illustration that the eyepiece is fastened to the last wire of the end covering; the hook-piece, however, is

How to Use the Shelter as a Table

FIGURE 8

The side and end panels must be in place and fastened with the hook and eye fastenings, when the shelter is in use as such. To use it as a table, or to make the bed, the panels can be removed.

Morrison "Table" Shelter

American Construction Battalions "CBs" were billeted in seafront hotels, bell tents on the Den and nissen huts at Courtenay Terrace. The Den Pavilion was their Mess where upwards of 2000 men took their meals in relays at long tables. The cookhouse was a temporary construction beside the Pavilion. Lots of children, myself included, got their first taste of ice cream after queuing outside the kitchen on Sunday mornings. During the week it was "Got any gum, chum?" - a request severely frowned upon by our parents. Father often arrived home from the Devon Arms with an American in tow from whom I had my first taste of banana, orange and Hershey bar. Early in 1944, the Americans started storing metal caissons on the Point car park. These six feet square boxes had metal rungs on all four sides, designed to allow them to be joined together with chains or wires. Guards, constantly on duty, never prevented us from using them as climbing frames. Hundreds of caissons were piled up eventually - 2 or 3 high. Early in June 1944 they disappeared overnight to be floated across to Normandy for use in the D-Day landings, not the famous Mulberry temporary harbour at Arromanches but 10 miles west in the American "Utah" sector where they became a floating road from ship to shore. It was destroyed by a gale four days later. We often listened to German propaganda wireless and at midnight on 10th January 1943 following the worst raid on the town, we were in our Morrison shelter listening to Lord Haw-Haw's "Jarmany Calling, Jarmany Calling". The first news item informed us "The great shipbuilding yard of Morgan Giles has been completely destroyed by German bombs." In fact, windows on the Strand side were shattered but nothing was seriously damaged. The Saxe St home of Marjorie Langworthy who "did" for my mother was bombed in that raid so she came to live with us for the duration. We rarely had less than 10 people in the house, sometimes more, during the war years. Our Morrison shelter in the kitchen was about 6'6" by 4' with the steel plate top supported by four legs made of 8-inch wide angle iron girders, joined together at floor level by 3-inch metal girders. A double mattress could be laid on its floor, a lattice of steel lathes. If the siren sounded or raids occurred close together, no less than 5 children occupied the mattress that was stored away with the wire mesh sides except when a warning sounded.

Our three evacuees and I spent every daylight hour of our school holidays in 1941 and '42 trundling a box cart round town to collect scrap metal and suchlike for the war effort. Dr de Vine's house on Den Crescent yielded an almost limitless supply of aluminium kettles, pots and pans as well as other goods. Our gleanings were taken to the Council Yard on Gales Hill and Councillor Irish commended us for the quantity collected. The box cart doubled as an excellent tank using a cardboard box for a turret and a broomstick for a gun. Creedy's had a receiving box for used razor blades with a sign to the effect that 10,000 blades would make a Spitfire. An optimistic hope - not only as far as quantity but the fact that Spitfires were constructed mainly of aluminium! Looking back at the eradication of the old town centre, we always used to comment that it had been gutted like a fish. My own first home, 11 Fore Street, was one of the many perfectly liveable homes to be destroyed by town planners, who did more damage to Teignmouth, in many people's opinion, than Hitler ever did.

Ken Boyce with Amusements in Spray Point tea gardens where the Bow family spent time in the 30s

When war broke out, the Durham Light Infantry jettisoned all the Boyce's equipment before they could get there to clear it

Eva Breed nee Dodd

In 1942, my friend Betty and I were in bed at 55 Bitton St. The siren went off but we took no notice and tried to go back to sleep. We heard a plane and got out of our beds to look out of the window and saw a plane flying low towards St James Church. It seemed close enough to touch if I opened the window. It disappeared then the whole street lit up, just like daylight. Then there was a very loud noise. We jumped back from the window and lay flat on the floor. The noise went on for quite a while. Lots of stuff fell on us but it didn't seem heavy. Then it went very quiet. I looked up and saw the sky through a hole in the roof. We discovered that the door had been blown across the staircase and the only way out was to slide across it. When daylight came, we looked at our bedroom and found that one bed was covered in six inches of rubble, the other broken in two by big rocks that had fallen on it. We lived with an aunt until we found another house. I feel very lucky to have escaped injury.

Bomb damage in Willow St near Eva's home

Audrey Lynne MBE

Leading a post war parade in Exeter

**Teignmouth Division
of Red Cross**

Commandant Miss A Lynne MBE sixth from R. Wartime service medals were displayed when visiting dignitaries assembled outside the pier

BRITISH RED CROSS SOCIETY

Miss Lynne of Clarina Cottage, Exeter St joined Devon/106 Detachment of BRCS in 1916. After the First War she became deeply involved with fund raising for a new voluntary Teignmouth Hospital to be built on the Barnfields Estate at Mill Lane. In 1939 she controlled Teignmouth's First Aid Post serving as Administrative Commandant from 1940-45. Her involvement continued into the 1960s and fellow member Gladys Webber recalls her as a great disciplinarian. Miss Lynne's years of endeavour were recognized when she was awarded an MBE.

Doris Knox

Doris Knox served in Devon/106 detachment and when Teignmouth Hospital was bombed in 1941, she and her colleague Amy Wickham crawled in under the rubble to

Blessing of Red Cross Ambulance outside St Michael's Church, 1940s. Doris Knox (R)

help the survivors until the Rescue Team could dig their way through to release them. In February 1946, the women received a letter from BRCS County Director.

"It affords me great pleasure to inform you that the BRCS Distinguished War Service certificate has been awarded to Mrs Doris Knox and Mrs Amy Wickham for their courage and devotion to duty on the occasion of the destruction of Teignmouth Hospital by enemy action on 8th May 1941 thereby greatly facilitating the work of rescuing patients and removing the bodies of those killed".

In June 1946 the women travelled to Buckingham Palace for the award of certificates made by the Queen.

BRITISH RED CROSS SOCIETY

Patron:
HIS MAJESTY THE KING.

President:
HER MAJESTY THE QUEEN.

Chairman of the Council:
H.R.H. THE DUKE OF GLOUCESTER, K.G.

Chairman of the Executive Committee:
The Hon. Sir ARTHUR STANLEY, G.B.E., C.B., M.V.O.
The Rt. Hon. LORD WOOLTON, P.C., C.H., D.L.

DISTINGUISHED WAR SERVICE

The Council of the British Red Cross Society record their high appreciation of the Services rendered by

Doris, Mrs Knox.

Woolton

26th June, 1946.

Chairman of the Executive Committee.

Joyce Rodwell nee Mole

Joyce was born in 1928 at School House on Brook Hill where her grandparents Densham were Caretakers. Her father was Superintendent of St John Ambulance and in her teenage years she joined the Red Cross Station at Park St, training under Miss Lynne and Mrs Knox. When she was 17, Joyce achieved the highest examination results ever recorded in the Totnes Red Cross Division.

Red Cross Station (R) Park St 1950s

Eileen & Bernard Brook

In the garden of The Grotto, Dawlish Rd, home of Bernard's grandmother.

An underground passage connecting the garden with Eastcliff House opposite was used as a shelter during air raids. At Christmas '42, Bernard's young niece Valerie Davies and her brother and sister in Bishopsteignton were thrilled to receive gifts he'd made from timber collected from local bombsites. Eileen and Bernard, their 20 month old son John and Bernard's teenage brother Edward died when their home in Alexandra Terrace was destroyed during Teignmouth's worst raid, 10th January 1943.

YOUR FOOD IN
WAR-TIME

PUBLIC INFORMATION
LEAFLET   NO. 4

Read   this   and
keep   it   carefully.
You   may   need   it.

Issued from the Lord Privy Seal's Office July, 1...

---

existing shops would receive these licences.   New shops would not be opened unless there was a need for them.

Shopkeepers would be instructed that they must not supply excessive quantities to any of their customers, and powers would be taken to prevent people from buying more than their reasonable share.

Maximum prices would be fixed by the Ministry for each controlled food, and would be shown clearly in the shop windows.

RATIONING SCHEME

Certain foods, soon after the outbreak of a war, would be brought under a rationing scheme similar to that which was introduced during the latter part of the Great War.   In the first instance, rationing would be applied to five foodstuffs—butcher's meat, bacon and ham, sugar, butter and margarine, and cooking fats. Later, it might be necessary to add other articles.

The object of this scheme is to make certain that foodstuffs are distributed fairly and equally and that everyone is sure of his or her proper share.

Before rationing begins application forms would be sent through the post to every householder, who would be asked to give particulars of everyone living in his home.   These forms, when filled in, would be returned to the local food office set up by the local Food Control Committee, which would issue the Ration Books, one for each person.

You would then register at a retail shop of your own choice for each rationed food.   This registration is necessary to enable the local committee to know the quantities of rationed foods which each shop would require.   There is no need to register with a shop in peace time.   It is not advisable to do so.

The Ration Books would have coupons, a certain number for each week.   The Ministry would decide how much food each coupon represented, and you would be entitled to buy that amount. In the case of meat, the amount would be expressed in money. Thus, you could choose between buying a larger amount of a cheaper cut, or a smaller amount of a more expensive cut.   In the case of other foods, the amount would be by weight.

For children under six years of age, there would be a Child's Ration Book, but the only difference would be that a child would be allowed half the amount of butcher's meat allowed for a grown-up person.   On the other hand, the allowance for a heavy worker will give him a larger quantity of meat.

For catering and other institutions, special arrangements will be made.

These are the plans for our national housekeeping in war time.   Like all plans for our civil defence they need your help. In war time there would be no food to waste, but with your care and co-operation we shall have enough.

Any enquiries about food supplies in war time should be addressed:—
The Director, Food (Defence Plans) Department, Great Westminster House, Horseferry Road London, S.W.1.

51—4382 1

BROOK HILL SCHOOL

Reception Class Children of Teignmouth Infants School July 1940.
Brook Hill houses to rear

On Wednesday 2nd September 1942, with a new school year underway, four FW 190s flew in from the southeast at about 150 feet and carried out a daylight raid on Brook Hill and Myrtle Hill. It happened only moments before the ringing of the end of day bell and 300 infants and juniors were still in their classrooms. Miraculously, despite death and destruction all around, every child survived. Beyond the school boundary, eight deaths were recorded and 33 injuries. Five properties nearby were destroyed and 160 seriously damaged. Many families moved away from town, attendance at the school diminished, and the Junior and Infant schools merged. Mr Whitear was the Headmaster, a post he held for many years. St James Parish Hall was used for some classes and the infants shared a large classroom at the senior school. During the upheavals, the staff helped load furniture and equipment into lorries and took turns at fire-watching in the damaged buildings.

Sixty years on, Jean Potter nee Palmer, a pupil at the time of the raid organized a

Staff of Teignmouth Infants School
July 1940

L-R Miss Price : Miss Best : Headmistress Miss Hayman : Miss Prowse : Joan Cutcliffe

Survivors' Reunion on the site of the school, now occupied by a supermarket. More than fifty pupils shared a joyous get-together, one or two travelling hundreds of miles to meet up with the majority who still live locally. They were delighted to be reunited with three former teachers including Doris Pidgeon whose 23rd birthday coincided with the raid. After being presented with a special cake for her 83rd birthday at the reunion, Doris recounted her impressions. Several others followed suit, recalling the terror yet the relief of survival during that unforgettable time. Another member of staff, Joan Mundy nee Cutcliffe who had been injured during the raid produced some photographs and has kindly permitted their inclusion in this volume. BBC Spotlight featured the event on local television and the author made a video record for The Wilson Archive

BROOK HILL SCHOOL

Brook Hill Staff May 1945

L-R Back row Doris Pidgeon : Miss Oliver : Mr G Whitear : Miss Short : ?
L-R Front row ? : Miss Reddaway : Headmaster Mr JC Whitear :
Miss Best : Miss Price

Jean Hirst nee Wilcox

Jean, born in Mill Lane in 1933 was a pupil at Brook Hill School during the raid in September '42. The siren sounded as her class was demonstrating its skills in Physical Education to a school Inspector. The teacher shouted the pre-arranged signal that sent the children scurrying to the school's underground shelter.... "Rabbits!" but Jean and her friend rushed instead to the domed roof surface shelter in the playground close to the steps down into Bickford Lane. The panicking girls were between the blast wall protecting the entrance and the door at the moment the bomb exploded about 25 feet away from them. They were covered in shattered cement and dust but otherwise unscathed.

BROOK HILL SCHOOL

60th Anniversary Reunion 2nd September 2002
L-R Back row Joan Mundy nee Cutcliffe : Doris Pidgeon L-R Front row Sally Crispin nee Such : Jean Potter nee Palmer, Reunion Organizer

Pat Isaac nee Whiteway

I was at the reunion on 2nd September 2002 marking the 60th anniversary of the bombing raid. It was an afternoon of nostalgia, tears and laughter and it was wonderful to meet my old school friends again, most of whom I had not seen for 55 years.

I remember the day of the raid vividly. I was terrified when the bombs were falling because only a few weeks earlier, my parents house next to the Gospel Hall graveyard in Grove Avenue had been severely damaged when Gloucester Rd was bombed. It had to be pulled down for safety, leaving only the front wall standing. When the raid began on the school, my only thought as both my parents were working, was to run to my grandparents at 8 Higher Brook St. I was in Miss Stone's class on the top floor of the school and ran down all the stairs to the basement and out into Bickford Lane leading to Higher Brook St. The ARP warden would not let me through so I ran all the way up Shute Hill, across West Lawn and down Exeter Rd (now Exeter St) where I met Joan Hill's mother. She said she had better take me. It was horrifying to see Higher Brook St in such a terrible mess. My grandparents house was still standing but all the adjoining houses were gone and buildings were still falling.

My grandparents lost many friends that day including next door neighbours Mr & Mrs Williams and Mrs Best and Pauline Best, the mother and sister of one of our school teachers Miss Hilda Best. Looking back, I realize it was stupid to run but I was only 9 and simply followed my reactions. My weeping mother eventually arrived after being

Brook Hill School shortly before demolition in 1975

told that nobody could find me at the school. She had feared the worst but when I emerged from the back room, all I got was a wallop!

When the Town Hall was bombed, all the windows and doors of the rooms we rented in a large house in Higher Brimley were blown in. Eventually we rented a house in Grove Crescent and this also suffered with windows and doors blown in and ceilings down after the raid in January 1943. My mother refused to move again so the glass and rubble was cleared and we remained in that house until our original house in Grove Avenue was rebuilt after the war. Sadly, it was demolished when the new Exeter Rd was built.

I think as a child to have lived through so many bombing raids, you never forget. I can relive every one of them. May our future generations never know of such atrocity.

Jim Carlson

In Teign St, wearing trousers made from a blanket

Born in Saxe St in 1930, Jim's childhood memories include the time he was sitting on the table having his cut knees attended to when a raid started. Everyone rushed in under the stairs but he was left behind. When his mother came out and saw blood running down his chin she cried "Jimmy's been hit!" But the force of the explosion had made him bite his lip and tongue! He watched trials of midget submarines with his friends Tony Chapman, Joe Curry, Lionel Hill and Colin Parrish from Tank, the old name for the Fish Quay. Under Bobbett's Quay there was a big hole in the rocks and sometimes a lobster lurked there. One spring tide, he poked at the hole, saw something shiny and pulled out a tin of corned beef! Above the Beehive Inn in Bitton St, Jim saw a silver coloured twin-engine plane; its almost square fuselage appeared to be corrugated iron. The swastika stood out clearly. He ran home and just as he arrived, glass shattered all around. Their house had to be checked for safety. His sister told the Inspector there was nothing wrong with it but as she touched the window of the top bedroom, it immediately crashed down into the street! Jim and his three sisters settled into the defunct Commercial Inn in Fore St, Shaldon where today's mini market stands. Their father was a Skipper in the Merchant Navy and Jim's brother had been torpedoed and invalided out of the Navy. The first whistling bomb exploded in the playing fields at the Grammar School and next day, young Jim was in the crater looking for the whistle! At 4pm each day, the Harbour River Patrol towed the boom across the river mouth. Ernie Chapman, home on leave asked Jim to help him shoot prawn pots down near Babbacombe before it got dark. The outboard was put at a tilt and they shot out over the boom at full speed with Ernie shouting to the guards "We'll be back about midnight!"

Jim was smuggled into the cinemas by grownups working at the Lyceum (aka Bug House), Carlton and Riviera. Finding his way home in pitch black held no fears for him.

Once, in the Carlton Cinema, everything went dark so he lay on the floor, pulling the seat down as a shield during a hit and run raid. Bullets came through the roof leaving it gaping open with rays of sun shining in. An enemy plane forced down by Spitfires was brought to the Point car park as a novelty for people to pay and view to raise funds for the Russian Front. Jim waited till the guard looked away then quickly cut out the swastika with his pocketknife. He hid it in a window seat but his Mum noticed the vile smell it gave off so he swapped it for a piece of shrapnel. He remembers hearing the workforce at Morgan Giles shipyard say they would not go to work unless guns were installed on the seafront. The rails around the Point car park had to be cut to allow the muzzles of the Bofors guns to be tilted when planes came in low over the sea. It was believed that enemy pilots used the Riviera as a marker.

Jim's sister Maggie was travelling home from an Exeter munitions factory by rail when an enemy plane opened fire. The train waited in the tunnel until a Spitfire came over and shot it down a good way off Parson & Clerk rocks. This was a good spot for catching lobsters and when Ernie & Jim put pots there, they discovered a cave leading in to the railway line. Frogmen could have used it to blow up the line so they reported it and it was rapidly bricked up. After seeing the body of a 3 month-old baby wrapped in Blackout paper - two layers of brown paper with coat of tar, and the remains of a bomb victim, Jim learned in childhood to take the difficulties of life in his stride.

Bomb-damaged Carlton Cinema

Ernest Chapman AB

Ernie was born in Teign St in 1910. As a RN Reserve he was called up 2nd September 1939. After reporting to Portsmouth he was attached to armed merchant cruiser AMC California at Greenock. Formerly a 13,000-ton passenger ship of the Anchor Line, she was equipped for war with eight 6-inch guns. In October 1939 he was sent to Scapa Flow for gun training on the Royal Oak, built in Devonport 1914. They learned how to ram shells and charges of cordite up the breach of dummy loaders on the old battleship. Scapa was believed to be impregnable but one night U47 slipped in and torpedoed the Royal Oak and 838 lives were lost. Later, he went on Northern patrols up around Iceland and Greenland and was attached to Air Sea Rescue at the Isle of Man where there were no restrictions or rationing. Fate decreed that Ernie's life should be spared three times. In addition to the Royal Oak, a minesweeper he'd served on was sunk. In July 1943, AMC California, as part of a small troop convoy, was seriously damaged by air attacks off Portugal and sunk by British Destroyer HMS Douglas. " I was jammy," says Ernie who returned from the war to contentment working as a milkman and fisherman. Now in his 90s, his zest for life undiminished, he signals cheerful greetings to passers-by from his riverside window seat.

Peter Chave

I was born in Parson St in 1935. Whenever the siren sounded the first thing my dad did was to open front and back doors of our home at 15 Northumberland Place, to save the glass from being shattered. It was common practice for people to take shelter from a raid in anyone's house until the "All-Clear" was sounded. During one raid, our hall was filled with passers-by including a Mr Jennings, Harbourmaster of Alderney, his wife and their daughters Ursula and Brenda, grandmother Mme Putteaux and Wally, a terrified German shepherd dog. After fleeing from the Channel Islands, the family moored their boat on the back beach and we took them in as evacuees until it was safe for them to return home. Wally had impeccable manners and temperament but was so terrified when a raid took place that his owners reluctantly decided to have him put to sleep to save him from further stress. Mme Putteaux spoke only in French and never forgave the Germans for Wally's demise. She was in her mid 70s, about four and half feet tall and generally a very demure and sweet old lady but when the sirens wailed, she changed completely. Instead of taking cover in the Anderson shelter she picked up a rifle almost as tall as herself, donned a tin hat and marched out on the quay to take pot shots at enemy planes, swearing in French at the pilots as she did so. The rifle had quite a kickback and once, she was knocked over the wall into the river! Luckily, the tide was in and she fell into the moored sand barge, suffering a sprained ankle. I was six at the time and the fear associated with the war had not caught up with me. Instead of going to the shelter, I would rush to the front room window just to watch this amazing lady striding towards the New Quay in spite of the threat of a 'clip round the ear' if I didn't get into the shelter immediately.

We had a lucky escape when the Town Hall and Market Place were destroyed on 13th August 1942. The blast affected all the glass in our house and we ended up completely windowless. My mother was more annoyed to have our weekly butter ration ruined by shards of glass than by the fact that there was not a single pane undamaged. A Mr Williams who was renting a room with us had passed away during the afternoon and been laid out by my mother and the District Nurse as was accepted practice then. We had to vacate our house because of an unexploded bomb outside Davis's Café in Somerset Place and slept on the floor of Regia House in Teign St. During our absence, the house was ransacked and all our family photographs stolen. The robbers must have had a shock when they discovered Mr William's body lying in a coffin on the first floor!

Labrador Bay with famous hotel and dwellings at the top

All our class went to the shelter in the playground of Brook Hill School when it was bombed on 2nd September 1942. I hardly recognized my mother and baby sister in her pram when they came to meet me because they had sheltered in the Co-op bakery and were covered in flour. My mother's leg was covered in blood from shrapnel and for the first time, I felt really scared. We managed to reach my aunt's house in French St and shortly after this, moved up to Labrador to escape the bombs. We shared an asbestos bungalow called The Thorns with Arthur and Mary Tremlett. It gave us a good view of German planes as they swooped low over the water for a raid and I remember seeing an airman struggle in the fuel-soaked sea after being shot down. I also recall hearing the explosion of a landmine killing an enemy pilot attempting to climb the cliffs. The adults took turns to walk me in to school at Stokeinteignhead but I often ran away. The teacher would stand over us with a cane until we had eaten something she knew we wouldn't like. When it was Mary's turn to take me to school, we were machine-gunned as we walked along the flat piece of main road where there is now a car park overlooking Lyme Bay. We saw the pilot clearly as he flew towards us. Mary pushed me into a pile of stinging nettles and I was convinced they hurt more than a bullet! My father worked for coal merchants Matthew & Bennett in Orchard Gardens and was exempt from active service but served as an air raid warden. Whenever a raid finished we waited outside the bungalow to listen for him coming home across Shaldon Bridge. His was the noisiest motorbike in Devon but it was lovely to hear it and know that he was safe and my mother knew it was time to put the kettle on. We returned to Northumberland Place and had a wonderful street party in Somerset Place when my usually reserved parents amazed me by joining in the Hokey Cokey and Lambeth Walk. What a happy night that was to remember!

Wendy Cooke nee Hill

Wendy Hill and cousin Jill Symons
Teignmouth beach July 1945

My grandparents, Ernest and Ethel Illman owned and ran the Glendaragh Hotel in Barnpark Rd during the war. Their two daughters, Barbara and Nancy, married respectively Jimmy Symons and Wilfred Hill, the latter going on to form a partnership with Jimmy's brother Bill as Hill & Symons Builders Ltd. I was born in Alwyns Nursing Home in March 1940. My cousin Jill arrived six weeks later and the two families were always very close. Our mothers took us along the path leading to Cliff Walk, probably in August 1942. At a gateway overlooking fields with a view to the sea, my mother stood shielding her eyes to look out across the bay when she saw a plane flying in over the sea, heading towards us. They pushed Jill and me in under the thick hedge nearby and lay on top of us until the danger had passed. The path was strafed with machine gunfire and their fear for our safety communicated itself very strongly to me. I was only two and a half, yet still remember the incident clearly although my cousin Jill has no recollection of it. I even remember crying because my knees were covered in mud afterwards! Years later, my aunt told me their main fear was that they would be shot, leaving two little girls wandering about on their own near the cliffs.

My father Wilfred served in the Home Guard and was later sent to the Far East but did not see active service. Jill's father, Jimmy was a Gunner on HMS Exeter during the battle of the River Plate in December 1939. He came home to a hero's welcome and later served on the Malta convoys. Because of the severity of the bombing, my grandfather decided to give up Glendaragh and move us all to north Devon in 1942. Two years later, we returned to live in a large house in Ferndale Rd that was later divided between our two families. The half known as Seymour was the home of my stepmother Julie Hill for over forty years until her death in 2002.

Men of No 1 Teignmouth Platoon Home Guard including Wendy's father, Wilfred Hill centre, back row

Roy Crook

My parents and I lived on the outskirts of southeast London, enduring the Battle of Britain and numerous air raids. My father's firm decided to move to Torquay and in April 1941 we went to share a large house "Hailsham" in Ferndale Rd with two other couples working for the same firm. My bedroom had a bay window overlooking the sea from which I saw a glow in the sky to the southwest the night Plymouth was bombed and I felt we had come out of the frying pan into the fire. I started at Teignmouth Grammar School at the beginning of summer term 1941 and joined 3rd Teignmouth Scouts St James Troop. If the Scouts were part of parades through the town, they marched in advance of the ATC encouraged by Mr Thomas, French teacher at the Grammar School. My 13th birthday on 24th October 1941 coincided with the 11th raid on the town and the crater in the school playing fields was there for ages before being filled in. During the summer holidays in August '42, a friend and I were pushing our bikes up Breakneck Hill when we saw an FW190 with black crosses on it drop bombs on Teignmouth. As was quite often the case, the siren sounded when the raid was over, shortly followed by the All Clear. We turned for home and on approaching New Rd, ran into a swarm of feathers. The closer we got to town, the thicker the feathers. We were told the bomb had hit the emergency bedding centre.

Later in the war, I was woken up early by a roaring noise, shot out of bed and saw several Lancaster bombers approaching from a southerly direction. They flew in so low over our houses that the crew in the cockpit were visible. The morning news said they were returning from a multi bomber raid in Northern Italy. In 1945 we moved to 33 Exeter Rd close to St James Church. Months before D-Day, large crates began to appear on the promenade. They arrived over night and each day, more appeared until they occupied the whole of the seafront. These were stacked up to 10 or 12 feet high with walkways between. By D-Day, all the crates had gone - the logistics of this exercise must have been enormous. The only sign that they had been there were a few fragments of wood. I moved back to London to begin work in January '46. In March 2002, Cyril Coleridge, Robin Osborn and I had a wonderful reunion in Shaldon.

Promenade September 1944 with concrete tank trap (R)

Emma Dewey nee Hooper

Emma, born in Stanley St in 1924 served two or three times every week as a part-time member of the local NFS for 18 months. She manned phone lines from 7pm to 7am, based at the temporary Fire Station at County Garage, set up after the destruction of the station in Northumberland Place in 1942. Faded documents now provide a glimpse of the past when NFS women were issued with two blankets, one pillowcase, a greatcoat or raincoat, tunic or overall, one pair of socks and shoes, a steel helmet and one ski cap. All these items plus buttons, shoulder titles, badges, service chevrons and wound stripes were recalled at the stand down of part-time members in March 1945. They were permitted to retain artificial dentures, surgical appliances and Mark III respirator spectacles!

Qualified Firewomen of the National Fire Service under Station 18.C.2.R in 1944

Emma Dewey back row, far left. Mrs Rudd front row left. Other Teignmouth women are Joy Cockram (Back row, 3rd from R) Joan Broom (Row 3, 4th from L) and Maureen Day (Row 3, 2nd from R)

John Dewey

John was serving with the Queen's Royal Regiment when he married Emma in 1943. After an air raid in February 1942, the Devon Constabulary sent a letter to the CO.

"Thank you for the very valuable assistance rendered by the men under your command…they did their work well in manning the barriers thereby greatly lessening the strain thrown on the police, at the same time guarding much unprotected property. Thanks to Ptes Dewey, Dodd and Benson who did very good work in the releasing of trapped people with utter disregard to their own personal safety."

EVACUEES

The Brown family of 2 Bank St took in twelve evacuees. More than 60 years later, they are still in touch with Pat Penwill nee Brown.

Pat Penwill nee Brown

In 1941 I had diphtheria and spent five weeks in Torbay Isolation Hospital sharing a cubicle with another Teignmouth girl, 3 year old Sylvia Cornelius who was so ill that her Mum was allowed into the cubicle every day. The raid killing a family of 5 in Second Avenue had taken place and Mum was anxious I would worry about the bombing so she asked Mrs Cornelius not to mention it to me. Mum was only allowed to speak to me through the window. The following year the raid took place on Bitton Avenue whilst I was in the temporary hospital in Hermosa Rd visiting Monty, an evacuee of 7

From window of the Brown's home at 2 Bank St

with a broken arm. We dived under his bed and he kept saying, "Don't leave me Pat". The noise was horrendous and we were terrified. Beds were needed for casualties so all patients who could be discharged were allowed home and Monty came back with me. Casualties on stretchers were already on the marble floor of the hallway as we left. Social events were still enjoyed and Mum and I used to baby-sit for Lieutenant Commander and Mrs Gardiner's two young children at Withens, a large house at the junction of Higher Yannon Drive and Exeter Rd. I believe he was RN Officer in Charge, stationed at the Marina Hotel in Powderham Terrace. Mum and I spent 10 weeks in the autumn of '42 with Dad, on war work in Gloucester and Wiltshire.

If the siren sounded at night, Mum would get us all down into the passage inside the front door of 2, Bank St. We were not allowed to have a shelter because we did not have a ground floor room. One of the evacuees "Jeep", always refused to join us saying that he would rather come down with the house than be buried with three floors of building on top of him. Twelve evacuees stayed with us during the war. Over 60 years later, I keep in touch with all of them.

I attended South Devon Technical College 1943-45 and worked for 10 weeks in the summer of '44 at Burtons Stores opposite the London Hotel. My work included

counting food coupons, cutting up, weighing and wrapping two ounces of this or that and going to the bank, all for 30 shillings a week! On the evening of VE Day, members of the church youth club and many others linked arms for an exuberant parade through the town doing the Palais Glide, Lambeth Walk and singing our heart out as we went!

Pat Brown (R) and Doreen Swinney beside anti-tank defence on slope to beach, foot of Mere Lane

EVACUEES

Evacuee John E Privett "Jeep" evacuated to Teignmouth Grammar School from Haberdasher Aske's School

John Harvey

Random recollections include clutching a few belongings in a bicycle bag and informing my mother she must not cry followed by the long train journey to Devon, a great event in my young life. Arriving at Teignmouth along with Michael Brenton and walking through the dark streets before finding a welcoming light and the kindly face of Mrs Brown at 2 Bank St. She took two lost souls under her wing and made them feel a little safer in a strange world. Her daughter Pat, a very senior 11 years old to my young eyes, must have had her world turned upside down by our arrival but she coped well. The beach was fenced as far as the eye could see with scaffolding poles to keep out the enemy....nasty people who either wore strange helmets or looked like Hitler. The Den was an inviting stretch where small boys spent many happy hours exploring and trying not to get into too much mischief. Bicycles could be hired for sixpence a half an hour from a shop nearby which invariably ran out of child's sized bikes so we rode on the crossbar. An armoured personnel carrier complete with bren gun was stationed on one of the Den pathways, no doubt to hold off advancing hordes should the need arise.

EVACUEES

We saw motor torpedo boats built in Morgan Giles shipyard being tested offshore and ME109s streaking down the river towards the sea firing at us before heading out over the Channel. We had happy times at 2 Bank St and found Mr Brown formidable but kindly. I used to go downstairs to the front door to get the milk, brought round by horse and cart and ladled straight from churns into jugs. Occasionally we had the treat of going to a small shop nearby for a pennyworth of ice cream but supplies were very limited. Details have blurred but the abiding impression is of a feeling that we were happy in our small way, well fed and looked after. My wife and I meet up with Pat and Albert 3 or 4 times every year.

Michael Brenton

I was not quite 7 in September 1939 when it was decided to evacuate the whole school. My mother had to say goodbye to her only child outside the school where we boarded a bus not knowing where I was going or when she would see me again. I said cheerily "Goodbye Mum….see you when the war is over!" and went off with my little bag of essentials, gas mask and a label around my neck. I can't recall the journey but remember being taken with John Harvey around Teignmouth in the dark by a lady trying to persuade several people to take us in. We arrived at 2 Bank St. Mrs Brown later told my mother that she had said she could take no more evacuees as she already had several but when she saw John and me on the doorstep, her heart melted and she could not turn us away. We were well treated and fortunate to be looked after by such a kind lady. I remember trying hard to learn to whistle and eventually succeeded standing by myself at a railway bridge. Afterwards, they could not stop me whistling wherever I went - I still whistle a lot! I fell into the boating lake and sat on the wall to wring out my socks. When King George VI was due to pass in the royal train, we waited in the park by the railway lines but were disappointed not to see him since the train flashed by at high speed. Mother came and stayed for several weeks. The beach was covered with anti-invasion devices and I cannot recall going on the sands at all. Soldiers were being drilled along the sea front. One of them spoke to the children but got shouted at by the Sergeant and we all felt sorry for him. Our schooling was in St Michael's Church House. Several classes were held in the one hall with the headmistress's table in the corner. I left around 1942 and cannot recall saying goodbye and going home but have happy memories of this period in my life. Pat Brown attended my 21st birthday and my wedding over 40 years ago.

EVACUEES

Peter Cooper

Just after D-Day in 1944, VI rockets started coming across the channel to Essex where I was at school in Chigwell. It was decided to close down early in July for the summer holidays. In August I found myself on a train as an evacuee going to Teignmouth. After the formalities were complete I arrived on the doorstep of 2 Bank St. I was made very welcome, stayed for a year and attended the Grammar School. I was used to a boys' only school and had been learning German and French but here, the stream I was in did not do French. It was all a bit different but I soldiered on and joined the ATC 60 Sqd. I felt quite smart in my uniform, marching through town on parades and it may have helped when I joined the RAF for National Service. I also joined the local Scout troop and remember climbing down a rope from Shaldon Bridge into a dinghy. When I think of it now, we must have been crazy as the tide was about to turn and I was petrified. After we were all in, we rowed up river for a campfire meeting with others. During the holidays, I helped fishermen with their rowing boat trips and saw the navy working on 2-man midget subs. We spent a lot of time on the beach and amusement arcade on the pier.

After the American troops vacated the seafront hotels, we collected water bottles and odd pieces of kit as souvenirs. I went to midnight mass with Pat at Christmas 1944 and opened my presents afterwards. The bedroom ceiling fell down on top of me one night. Mr Brown was away on war duty as a civilian at Padstow and could not get back to prepare another bedroom so I camped on the floor. That winter we used bits of corrugated iron sheet to snowboard down Little Haldon. I joined St Michael's Church choir and got a holiday job as a delivery boy on Mudge's bakery van calling at various hotels round town and did odd jobs in the bake house on Saturday mornings. My mother came down when she was able and the Browns became my second family. VE Day and night will always stay in my memory with everyone celebrating, marching round town and having the time of their lives! My one regret was the fact that my education faltered over the languages and on returning to my old school for the final years, I never really caught up and failed my school certificate. Compared to what others suffered and lost, my loss was minimal and I made up for it by studying at night for my professional qualifications. Looking back, apart from feeling a little homesick from time to time, the year went very well.

Grammar School ATC 60 Squadron 1944
Peter Cooper (Evacuee) Front row 3rd from R

Sarah Farleigh nee Ridd

Born in 1912, Sarah was working as a housemaid in Barnsley House when her sister said there was more money to be made repairing Spitfires at Newton Abbot. A commercial garage on Totnes Rd had been taken over for this vital work. Sarah learned how to strip down damaged aircraft riddled with bullet holes and cover any exposed wires with tape. Next she had to fit new fabric painted in red foul smelling "dope". When raids on Teignmouth became frequent, her family moved to Ashwell, west of Bishopsteignton from where Sarah walked in to work and caught a bus home. She became so adept at the techniques that she was sent to train women newly engaged in similar work at Plymouth. It coincided with heavy raids on the city so she  returned home after two weeks. In 2002 Sarah continues to walk every weekday to the Alice Cross Centre where she celebrated her 90th birthday with many friends.

Sylvia Forrow nee Wreford

As England declared war on Germany in September 1939, I began my first term at Teignmouth Grammar School. We caught the 8.30 am school train each morning, pulled by good old steam engines. It was never more than a minute or two late regardless of war or rough seas breaking over the line. In the early days, we carried gas masks in cardboard boxes wherever we went. On the way to school we called at Beatty's sweet shop before it was bombed. The school windows had been taped to protect us from flying glass and Blackout curtains covered the windows and doors. Trenches had been dug in the school field but I only remember sheltering in them once. Later, when the siren went, we had to cross the road and shelter in the cellars of the big houses in Landscore Rd. Miss Stockley always used to produce a tin of biscuits! This arrangement was impractical particularly as the raids were usually a quick "tip and run". The siren didn't go off until after the bombs were dropped, followed quickly by the "All-Clear". In May 1941 when the hospital was bombed, the headmaster, Mr Silverston was very upset when he told us all at Assembly that Beatrice James had been killed in the raid. She had only recently left the school to take up her career in nursing. Pupils from Haberdasher Aske's Schools in London were evacuated here. The organization must have been brilliant as all the facilities had to be shared yet school life went on as usual. A dozen Jewish refugee children also joined our school. Each morning they held their own service whilst we attended Assembly in the school hall where the walls were covered with posters identifying German and British planes.

**The Grammar School's new Assembly Hall completed in 1938 had
to absorb many extra pupils when Haberdasher Aske's London
School pupils were evacuated to Teignmouth**

A highlight of the year was the Eisteddfod organized by Mr Thomas. The three houses of Teign, Dart and Exe competed strongly with one another in every aspect of sport, music, and drama.

One October evening of 1941, a school social was in full swing when bombs fell close by killing two people and injuring five others. One bomb landed on the edge of our hockey pitch and the crater was still there when I left school some years later. We juniors, sent home early from the social, were waiting on the platform for the 9.15 train home when the raid began. The station and the train were blacked out and it was scary in the pitch dark. It was a relief when the noise stopped, the All Clear sounded and the train pulled away towards Dawlish at last. During another raid, we heard the sound of cannon fire very close and dived under our desks. A row of bullet holes was later discovered in the wall of Mr Silverston's study by the school's front entrance. We arrived in class one day in '42 to find Sheila Hamlyn's desk empty. Sheila and other members of her family had been killed in a raid. On Sunday 10th January 1943, I acted as a "casualty" with my friend Beryl Davey in a big Civil Defence exercise and from Dawlish seafront we heard gunfire and bombing over Teignmouth. Suddenly, two planes came diving in from behind Lea Mount. An FW 190 was being chased by one of our planes. Guns blazed and the FW's fuselage was hit. It crashed into the sea with a big splash and our plane was so low that it flew through the fountain of water. We later learned that it was one of seven planes that had caused Teignmouth's worst raid.

In the middle of school certificate exams, we went up on to the school field and saw all the vessels setting out to sea for D-Day. They were exciting years yet school life carried on relatively normally. Our light relief was from evening wireless programmes such as Tommy Handley in ITMA and Lord Haw-Haw was always good for a laugh!

Tel. Jack French DSM

W/T Office, Hong Kong August 1949

Jack lived in Teign View Place in the late 1930s and played a significant role in the war between Chiang Kai Shek's National Army and Mao Tse Tung's Communist Army. In April 1949, four Royal Naval ships, HMS Amethyst, London, Consort and Black Swan gathered in the waters off Shanghai. Jack was Telegraphist aboard the Amethyst, ordered to relieve Consort and take supplies to the beleaguered British Embassy in Nanking. Amethyst proceeded up the Yangtse River but came under artillery and small arms fire from the Communist Army. Several crew were killed including the Captain and Medical Officer. The ship continued to defend herself despite severe damage and further casualties until direct hits on both the bridge and wheelhouse caused her to run aground. It was decided to evacuate the ship to prevent further casualties and it was re-floated during the night, leaving Jack as the only Communicator aboard. For the following six days, he went without sleep, assisted by Benzedrine, until contact was made with the local Communist Commander. Jack was awarded an immediate DSM and ordered to rest. The crew were incarcerated for 100 days during unsuccessful negotiations for a free passage. After running short of food and oil, the ship made her escape under the cover of darkness on 31st July 1949. Thwarting artillery fire, block ships and barrier nets, Amethyst reached Hong Kong on 2nd August.

Jack French was popular with his shipmates and was renowned for his taste for a matelot's delicacy of herrings in tomato sauce, generally known as "herrings in". He is described as a modest man who truly lived up to the high tradition of the Royal Navy. His awards include the Naval General Service medal granted for service in foreign wars, with the Yangtse Bar in 1949.

William Gallin

During the war years, Bill manned Teignmouth Telephone Exchange every evening from 8pm to 8am, seven days a week. Self-dialling telephones were not available and at that time, callers had to lift the phone and wait for the operator to connect them with the required number. Air raid warnings were sent through to Teignmouth Exchange from Exeter and the operator passed these messages on to the headquarters of wardens, police and fire brigades. These in turn telephoned their outposts, again via the operator. In the event of bombs falling, reports from the various services would come into central control from where orders were sent to alert the personnel and order equipment required

to deal with the damage. Every single call went through the Exchange, creating a considerable amount of work. Bill held a set of keys that could restrict the telephone lines to those used only by the emergency services. He never operated the keys, reckoning that if members of the general public were anxious to find out if relations and friends were safe, they would be worried if they were unable to obtain an answer from the telephone. Bill handled the calls with speed and efficiency, enlisting the aid of his son Jack and daughter Doris from their living quarters above the Post Office. Priority was given to emergency numbers and although there was some delay, every call was answered and connected. When an unexploded bomb was discovered nearby and all adjoining properties evacuated, Bill continued to man the Exchange even though the bomb was only a few yards away.

Joyce Garside nee Nicholson

Women's Auxiliary Air Force

I was born in Saxe St in 1923. Just before the first raid in 1940, I was walking down Mill Lane with my friend Ivy when we saw a plane and it was making an unusual noise. It dropped two bombs and people came running from their houses to see what had happened. A little while later, a car passed us on the hill with our great friend Joyce Medland on the back seat. We did not realize she had been injured and was being taken to hospital by car since there was no ambulance then. We were so sad when Joyce died from injuries the next day.

One evening, Ivy and I saw two men in Brunswick St and thought it suspicious when we heard them say they were going to film the river at midnight when the moon was full. We knew nothing about spies but after the war, I remember Mr Williams of Tozers saying there were lots of spies around here and when raids were on, they hid on Haldon.

Many people moved away from Teignmouth when the bombing got bad. My parents stayed on, father working at Morgan Giles shipyard where MTBs were being built. I shall never forget seeing a six year old girl dug out in Bitton Avenue, wrapped in a blanket lifeless and laid on the pavement. I volunteered for war work and was sent to Exeter with Winnie Lewis also from Teignmouth and trained to make aircraft parts in a Gandy St workshop, close to the Museum. In May 1942 we were on night shift. I hadn't heard that Hitler had ordered Exeter to be destroyed or I might not have gone up! We were ordered to shelter in the basement of the University when the bombing started. High explosives and incendiaries rained down and one landed by the side of the Museum but failed to explode. Incendiary bombs later destroyed the workshop. All transport had ceased and we had to walk to Exminster to board a train for home. By the time I got back, Mrs Hook, having lost her son and family, had been to commiserate with my mother as they had heard I was missing.

On Sunday 3rd January 1943, I had tea with Eileen and Bernard Brook and their little son. Eileen had read in the paper that the war would soon be at an end. One week later, they lost their lives in their home in Alexandra Terrace. I joined the WAAF and after serving on a Maintenance Unit for a while, served just over two years at RAF St Mawgan.

For many years now, Joyce has dedicated herself to collecting for the Wings Appeal of RAFA's Benevolent Fund and is proud to have been made an Honorary Life Member of the Teignmouth Branch RAFA Association.

Roy Geary

I was born here and as a small boy lived in Teign St on the corner of Sun Lane. I often went along the river beach and down to the Point with a friend and when we were between Lifeboat House and the toilets, an enemy plane flew in over the Ness heading towards Dawlish. It strafed the area with shellfire as we dived for cover next to a wall that had been built to block off the lower level car park. We were lucky to escape injuries. I was watching rolls of barbed wire for defensive purposes being off-loaded from a lorry near a wall, built to block the slipway beside Bobbetts Quay. One went awry and rolled into my leg causing a nasty gash. I spent 3 days in bed in a darkened room and still have the scar! In those days you could walk right through Devon Arms Yard where, prior to the 1944 Invasion, maintenance was done on American vehicles with the distinctive 5-point white star on the side. I asked one of the servicemen the inevitable question "Got any gum, chum?" and was taken over to their Mess in the Den Pavilion and given jelly and ice cream!

On the afternoon of 10th January 1943, I was on my way to the Gospel Hall Sunday School when the siren sounded. A bomb entered the upper storey of the building just across the road and I saw it come out the other side and bounce on the paving stones. (See page 114 of Teignmouth at War 1). I sheltered against the wall as we had been taught; my head tucked down between my knees, and was caught by flying glass from the window of Shaw's fish and chip shop opposite home. My name was added to the official records of people injured during raids. We moved out to Holcombe and lived next door to Mr Sims, a toy and puppet maker. Some of my happiest hours were spent watching him carve wood and create papier-mache puppets, many of which were sent abroad. I believe he made the first Archie Andrews dummy and when I think of him now, it seems he was the living image of Pinocchio's creator in the Walt Disney film. I served in the Royal Navy from 1953-63. Apart from those ten years, I have lived in the same place for the past 45 years and really love Teignmouth.

Bowling Club and Den Pavilion Winter 1947

The Brunswick Press produced a Christmas card to be sent to all those serving King and Country

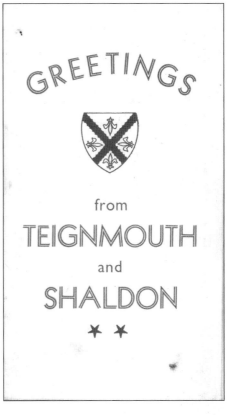

GREETINGS

from

TEIGNMOUTH

and

SHALDON

✱ ✱

Best of Luck to YOU from your Home Town. St Peter's Shaldon, T&S Baptists, Gospel Hall, T&S Congregationalists, St James, St Michael's, Salvation Army, T&S Methodists and Our Lady & St Patrick sent messages of encouragement.

Mr H Irish, Chairman of Teignmouth Urban District Council wrote "At this season of the year, we, your friends in Teignmouth send our sincere greetings. Our thoughts go out to you continually and we look forward to the time when by your work and sacrifice you will be repaid by bringing in an Era of Real Peace, and we shall be able to gladly and thankfully welcome you home.

The final message was from the Man in the Street – John Citizen: These greetings come from your parents, wives and families, brothers, sisters and sweethearts where ever you may be on Land, Sea or Air, in hospital or prisoner of war. Never forget that though there may be delays in your Mails, remember you are always in their Thoughts and Prayers, so keep smiling.

Philip Charles Gourd 3rd Battalion Coldstream Guards

The most brutal massacre of the western war took place in the area of Monte Sole, Italy on 30th September 1944. Philip Gourd of Bishopsteignton was serving with the 3rd Battalion Coldstream, advancing towards the Gothic Line. Ahead of them were hamlets including San Martino and Casaglia, each with its little church and walled cemetery where civilians sought refuge. The 16 SS, retaliating against Partisan action, machine-gunned and bayoneted everyone in sight. Nearly 1800 civilians of all ages were slaughtered over a period of weeks.

On the 50th Anniversary of the massacre of Monte Sole in 1994, the Archbishop of Bologna conducted a service of commemoration in Marzobotto where a Crypt Mausoleum for the massacred exists outside its church. Former combatants including Intelligence Sgt Gourd were presented to the Archbishop and the President of the Republic of Italy. The now silent mountain is a Peace Park devoid of houses and people and will remain so with only the ruined buildings as unspoken witness to the dreadful fate of their occupants. In 2002, Philip wrote an article on this subject for the Monte Sole magazine, distributed across Europe. A former German soldier from the mountain regiment that took over from the SS at Monte Sole read the article and wrote to Philip in perfect English, expressing his hope that ex-enemies could now be friends. Italian film Director Bonicelli believes the world should be told the story of Monte Sole and plans to make a Docu/Drama in September 2002.

John Hayman

When war was declared I was not quite four years old and my parents tried to shield me from what was happening. I remember feeling privileged to be given a Mickey Mouse gas mask, immensely more appealing than the plain masks, an unusual toy rather than a grim warning about what might happen. My sister, almost three years older, did not qualify for such a mask and her memories of preparation are less playful. She remembers father taping the floorboards and living room windows against a gas attack and worried silently about what would happen when one needed to go to the lavatory. Unprepared as I was, the first air raid I recall was perhaps as a result, the more frightening. On the afternoon of 7th July 1940 as a single plane dropped five bombs, my mother and I sheltered in a dark, windowless passage in our house. She may have meant to keep us from shattering glass or perhaps this was as close as we could get to a cave. I don't think there had been a siren warning. Often it sounded as the first bombs fell, its seemingly anxious, piercing wail fighting against the staccato of machine guns and the thud of bombs dropping. The "All-Clear" siren had a more melodious undulation but even as a child I wondered how the authorities could know the raid was over. Might there not have been another wave of bombers?

Later, during night raids we sheltered in the cupboard under the stairs. I was picked up in a muddle of bedclothes and carried downstairs to this confined space. My sister was considered old enough to look after herself and told to keep her slippers by her bed so she could run downstairs without cutting her feet on shattered glass. I was more protected than she was, in part by my limited awareness. The noise of the raids was more upsetting than the sense of imminent destruction. The closeness found with my sister, mother and teddy bear under the stairs was quite comforting.

This phase ended on 2nd September 1942 when I was six and my home and school were damaged during the same air raid. Again, there was no warning siren, just the shattering of glass from high windows, the thud and explosion of bombs, and the cry of a teacher "Under the desks!" The attack was brief and when it was over, we filed out to the bomb shelter in the playground. The raid occurred at 4 pm. Some people considered it was a miracle that we had not been released from school since the injuries and deaths from shrapnel, falling debris and machine gun fire would have been considerable. It was rumoured that one of the bombs had been defective and caused less damage than it might have done. As it was, the raid was devastating enough. Four bombers had each dropped a high explosive, killing eight people and damaging 160 properties.

My father, an air raid warden collected my sister and me from school and said, "We're alright but you must be prepared to find our house has been damaged." The school was less than 100 yards from our home. At least one bomb had fallen in this area and others had fallen on the far side of the school. I often wonder if my memory is inaccurate in its recollection of the row of terraced houses

Lower Brook St Cottages built by WH Hayman and demolished 1970s

opposite the school. I think of them as having their front walls neatly removed so one could see straight into a cross section of the two-storey homes, revealing all their tawdry furnishings and messiness. There seemed to be something quite indecent about this sudden loss of privacy, the feeling accentuated by a partly dressed woman crying out from the second floor bathroom. I thought it impolite to look closely…perhaps father told me not to. When I have doubted my memory, I wondered if I confused the appearance of these houses with my sister's doll's house. However, she has exactly the same memory.

We were not allowed to enter our damaged home. Our parents spoke of fallen plaster and broken glass and probably thought we would find it too upsetting. Father fetched some bedding and we carried these awkward bundles to the bus stop. The experience has become mixed up with other images…in this instance, with pictures of refugees. It is a completely misleading association because there was nothing desperate about our relocation but at the time I felt oddly dispossessed as if something quite disruptive was happening even though we were just taking a bus ride for a couple of miles to move in with my grandmother. Perhaps I was also vaguely aware that another, more personal change had come about in my life. Earlier, during night raids I had been bundled into bedclothes and carried to the shelter. Now I was suddenly old enough to carry my own bedclothes down the street! It was certainly an odd thing to do, but this new responsibility made me feel quite important!

Overview from St Michael's tower 1944. Brook Hill School visible beyond Hollands Rd and Station Rd

Len Hayter

Len joined the RAF in June 1939, training first as a Wireless Operator and later as an Air Gunner. Travelling to Newton Abbot in a car with his family a few days before the first air raid at Teignmouth, July 1940, an aircraft was suddenly spotted flying low over the river. They watched it head west towards Newton from their position close to the bend beyond the turning to Wear Farm. "Is it one of ours?" his father asked and, to avoid too many concerns, Len agreed that it probably was. They encountered a Policeman on point duty and he reported the sighting immediately to the Police Station. It may have been a reconnaissance trip by one of the first enemy planes to be spotted in this area.

Maggie Heywood

I was born in Teignmouth in 1946 and lived in the town until I was 21, retaining links there and returning six or seven times every year until my mother came to live with me in 1993 for her last four years. A photo on page 59 of Teignmouth at War 1 shows our home Peribank, Yannon Drive with my mother Biddy Heywood sorting through our possessions after the raid. My 4 year-old brother Graham was asleep in his cot upstairs when the bomb fell. The door and windows were all blown out by the blast and my parents thought he must have been killed because they couldn't hear any sound from upstairs. It took my Dad a little while to shift the rubble sufficiently to be able to get up the stairs but Mum couldn't bring herself to look. When he finally reached Graham's room he found the protective frame from around the windows had fallen across the cot and held most of the glass and debris and he was still fast asleep beneath it all!

As a family we knew the Hamlyns of 41 Bitton Avenue very well, although not at the time their house was bombed. Syd Hamlyn was serving with the army in Egypt when his wife and two daughters were killed in their home. He was distraught and took it very badly. Eventually he met a lovely person called Lily Drew who used to be our daily help. They married and I became a sort of surrogate daughter because they had no children of their own. The three houses on Bitton Avenue were rebuilt, Syd and Lily living at number 41 for the rest of their lives.

Lorna Howson nee Ridd

First uniform as a nurse in training at Teignmouth & Shaldon Hospital, 1935

Lorna had become a staff nurse by the time it was bombed in the early hours of 8th May 1941. Temporary accommodation for the next few hours was offered in Mrs Blewett's house just across the road from the hospital. The nurses were eventually relocated to Garland House, a semi-detached building where they had to cram into the lounge and the attic and share one bathroom. When Hermosa House was turned into a temporary hospital, the nurses walked up in their dressing gowns each day to use the facilities until more permanent quarters were established for them. After learning of the death of Doris Knox in 1984 (see British Red Cross Society section) Lorna wrote to Doris's son David.

" I shall always remember her extreme kindness to me and others after that fateful night when we lost 3 nurses and 7 patients so tragically. She took us to her house in the morning for breakfast and a cleanup. She helped us on many other occasions."

HERMOSA HOUSE HOSPITAL

After Teignmouth Hospital at Mill Lane suffered a raid in 1941, a temporary hospital was set up in Hermosa House on Landscore House. The wealthy land-owning Sweetland family built it in the mid 18th century and it served the community until the new hospital opened on Mill Lane in 1954. The old house was demolished and new homes built as Hermosa Gardens on the site.

**Matron with nurses on terrace of temporary hospital,
Hermosa House 1942/3**

(L-R and back row to front) Widger, Letheran, Causley, Pearson, Ridd & Oats

Hermosa House Hotel from the Lawns 1930s

HOOK FAMILY

William Edward "Wayne" Hook

Born in Teignmouth in 1908 and was a fisherman until the war when he served in RN River Patrol with his father. See the photograph, page 85 of Teignmouth at War 1.

Leslie George Hook AB

Born in Teignmouth in 1910, Leslie served on HMS Andania, an armed cruiser based on the Clyde. He was home on leave on 2nd March 1941 when an air raid occurred. Leslie and his wife Dorcas, daughter Delphine and his parents-in-law were killed at their home in Second Avenue. His brother Fred and the whole Guard of HMS Raleigh at Devonport attended the funeral in Teignmouth and walked in front of his coffin through torrential rain.

Leslie, Dorcas & Delphine Hook

Second Avenue after the raid on 2nd March 1941

HOOK FAMILY

Frederick James Hook AB

Fred was called up from RNR and joined an armed merchant cruiser HMS Andania, the same ship as his brother Leslie. On 16th June 1940, the ship was torpedoed and sunk by U-Boat UA south east of Iceland. An Icelandic trawler picked up all crewmembers. Fred was shore-based for the next 14 months then joined an O Class destroyer, HMS Offa in September '41 at its homeport, Scapa Flow. Whilst escorting Russian Convoys, the ship and its crew endured dreadful conditions including thick ice forming on the ship's interior and living quarters. They experienced many savage attacks from U-boats and enemy aircraft and were involved on the disastrous PQ17 convoy to Russia when the Ministry of Defence ordered the convoy to disperse, leaving merchant ships unprotected from attack. The convoy picked up survivors but there was dreadful loss of life. HMS Offa completed duties in Nova Scotia, Gibraltar, Casablanca, Sicily and Italy. During the Allied Invasion and subsequent surrender of Italy, they were off the coast in the ship that Fred left in December '43. He transferred to HMS Drake and joined HMS Antigua at Liverpool in June '45. In between he did an occasional week with Teignmouth's River Patrol under Captain Rees based at the Royal Hotel, code-named HMS Mount Stewart. Fred was demobilised in November 1945.

Sydney Charles Hook DSM BEM

Syd, born in Teignmouth 1920, turned his back on boat building and fishing and set off with 14 other young men by train for Exeter to join the Royal Navy at Christmas 1939. His first time at sea was with the patrol service on board a trawler from Hull as part of a North Sea escort. Next he trained in anti-submarine detection and bomb disposal where his officer inspired such confidence that his men saw little danger in their task. His unit quickly moved in after a 1000Kg bomb fell adjacent to a vital tower used for radio location (early radar) at Cleethorpes. Bombs normally lay untouched for around 100 hours before disposal but this one needed immediate attention because of the tower. It took 19 days to dig a pit large enough to expose the bomb that was eventually defused by compressed air.

HOOK FAMILY

Syd Hook (L) with fuse of 1000Kg bomb dropped at Cleethorpes

The Ross, a 710-ton Hunt Class fleet sweeper on which Syd was serving got straddled by three bombs and was towed into the Humber where fifty other minesweepers were based. Some of the ship's food was terrible and the dreaded mutton stew with an inch of fat on the top was called nuts and bolts! He sometimes fished for cod with a line from the deck of Chameleon, a mine spotting patrol ship. Syd's war began to hot up in August 1942 when he accepted a transfer as a shipwright and left the Clyde with 15,000 British and American troops aboard the Queen Mary. "It was like paradise to cross the Atlantic on a 3 funnel liner. We lived it up and enjoyed white bread and chocolate...and music! After four days at full steam, we arrived in Boston. Over a thousand men were billeted in Wells Fargo barracks. On Trafalgar Day, October 21st, we had a fine time at the Union Jack Club"

Unknown numbers of Landing Ship Tanks (LSTs) were being built all over the States. He joined LST 403, length overall approximately 310 feet with enough capacity to carry 30 Sherman Tanks on the main deck and up to 25 support vehicles on the upper deck. After trials it put to sea on 16th February 1943, forming part of an enormous convoy including 9 destroyers. An LST rolls like a pig but conditions on board were better than British ships and each man had his own bunk and locker. After 28 days they reached

HOOK FAMILY

Gibraltar. From the moment of arrival there was little respite from constant moving of troops, transport and equipment from point to point. Over a dozen different ports were serviced including Algiers, Bizerta, Tripoli, Bougie and Malta. Beside frequent air and submarine attacks, the crew were faced with constant shortages of essential equipment. Landings at a beachhead followed strict routine: all hands to Action-Stations start up tank space exhaust fans, open bow doors and half-lower ramp. If conditions were satisfactory, the vehicles were run off the main deck within half an hour. Those on the upper deck had to be brought down in the lift and this could take two or three hours. Enormous steel platforms (pontoons) were used whenever a false beach was encountered, and manned by very courageous seamen.

Syd recalls a lighter moment "A News Team came aboard to film 1500 prisoners, 21st Panzers, still armed with knives, we had to collect and take to Algiers. A cameraman got set up to film them as they marched down towards the ship whistling Lili Marlene. While his back was turned, we all had a go at filming and used up all the reel!" The gradual build-up of naval units began and early in July 1943, flotillas grouped at Bizerta to form the largest invasion fleet assembled up to that time. LST403 was at Cape Passaro for the invasion of Sicily. With intervening tactics from the fleet and air cover by the RAF that kept Focke-Wulf 190s at bay, the landing went well. Again at Reggio on 3rd September, they were virtually unopposed but it was a different story at Salerno where they encountered aggressive action from constant shell and bomb attacks and the first radio controlled glider bombs. The army's advance came to a halt north of Naples and another attempt to outflank the Germans was made at Anzio in January 1944. Over the following ten weeks, LST 403 made 18 trips to Anzio to evacuate wounded troops, civilians and PoWs. It also transported deadly cargoes of ammunition, land mines and petrol. Landings became increasingly difficult since the beachhead was being blown away by constant shellfire. Anzio was a head-on meeting with hell.

LST 403 was ordered back to Britain in April and Syd began practice for the Normandy Landings with the marines at Harwich. LST 403 left on 5th June 1944 and made a landing at Gold Beach. This went well due to good organization and once the Durham Light Infantry took the Beach, enemy fire was greatly reduced. The bodies of eighteen who lay dead in their overcoats were picked up and put in collapsible boats for proper burial. In all they made 6 landings and 17 trips between the English mainland and Normandy bringing back thousands of British troops and Prisoners of War. The PoWs were astonished to see so many buildings as they sailed up Southampton Water because they had been told that their bombing raids had flattened everything. LST403's final trip was on August 20th with 400 German SS Panzers herded in the tank space. As they were being brought up for disembarkation in the elevator about 40 at a time, a newly fitted cable tore free from its housing. The elevator catapulted down onto the tank deck, two Germans died and several others were injured including a Lieutenant

HOOK FAMILY

R. Carpenter. In later years, Lt Carpenter wrote that Shipwright Hook never lost his sense of humour and did more than anyone to keep LST 403 going through thick and thin.

Bringing the author up to date in 2002, Syd said that the last part of his service was at a Commando Camp on the Kent coast. "I had some good times and would rather have been in the war than stay in the boat building job I had first. The worst bit was Anzio and the best bit - New York!" and a memory-laden chuckle echoes round the cosy kitchen overlooking the Teign estuary.

Stanley Gordon Hook

Too young to join up, Stan served in the Home Guard.

Hook Family 1940

L-R Frederick James, William Edward (Wayne), Stanley Gordon, Leslie George, Sydney Charles,
Parents Elizabeth Ann and William Edward

Shirley Ingram nee Collins

In 1943, my parents and I were staying with my grandmother above Martins' shoe shop in Bitton St. Mother took over the running of it after Grandfather's death and father ran Marks Collins Bakery, almost next door. The siren sounded whilst I was attending Sunday School in St James Parish Hall on 10th January '43. We tried to shelter under a large table during the explosions that sounded very close. Soon afterwards, my father Roy who was an ARP warden appeared and told me he'd just had a lucky escape after a bomb bounced up Saxe St and exploded against the garage door at the rear of the bakery. He had been working on a van in the yard and had just gone indoors for dinner. Mrs Stowers, the Sunday School superintendent, took me to her house whilst my mother and grandmother packed a couple of suitcases. The three of us stepped over broken glass strewn along Bitton St and made our way out to stay with our friends the Churchills at Coombe Vale. My father spent the night with the Hammonds in Exeter St to be near the bakery where a fire broke out in the debris early next morning. Our bungalow at Coombe Vale had been let out so we lived at Glenholme on Yannon Drive. I shall never forget this time.

Shirley Collins with Aunty Mary Collins (L) cousin Marion, Freda Hammond and Jolly the dog, early 1940s

Colin Ingram, "Buster" to his family, beside their home in Shaldon's Middle St, 1944

Colin Ingram

As a boy during the war, I remember that Shaldon beach was lined with barbed wire defences with one or two openings to allow access to the ferry. I was playing there when we saw planes flying over at a very low level from the Newton Abbot direction. They began to machine-gun us and we dived under the jetty then ran to the ferry shelter. Grownups were sheltering under the seats so we ran across to the bakery and Miss Dunn sheltered us under the kitchen table until the All Clear. When a bomb fell on Shaldon, the fin caught on telephone wires above the Green and it bounced up to the allotments. I was having tea at the time. Our kitchen window was blown in and the table scattered with broken glass. My family still laugh when they remember how I sat picking the pieces out of my salad! Later, when I walked through the village streets they were ankle deep in glass. If the bomb had dropped on the Green it would have caused heavy damage and loss of life.

Anti-invasion barricades line Shaldon's beach

Trevor Jackson

I often wonder how my father felt in 1939 when war was declared. He had spent three winters in the trenches during World War One with all the carnage and inhumane conditions war involves, and the same thing was about to happen again 24 years later. All the sacrifices made by the young men of his generation had been wasted. Now he had a family of six boys to bring up – what a prospect! I was the fifth son and six years of age. We lived in Shaldon and my first clear memory was the arrival of a troop of Indian Cavalry. Billeted somewhere outside the village, they brought their horses to the blacksmith situated within the high sandstone walls of Middle St. Shortly after this, our beach was transformed by a mass of steel scaffolding erected to form a defence against the expected invasion in 1940. We used the barricade as a giant climbing frame. There were tank traps at the beach exits and steel structures along the river to prevent the landing of airborne troops on Salty or the upper reaches of the Teign. Anti-aircraft guns were placed at various points around the river and seafront, a rocket launcher to the east of the pier and there were two very large naval guns in front of Ness House. The whole village shook when these guns were fired in practice. I recall a report that one of the guns suffered a breach explosion and the entire gun crew were killed.

The first air raid came to Teignmouth on Sunday 7th July 1940. A lone German plane flew the length of the seafront, turned and to the surprise of the many people out for a stroll along the prom, dropped two bombs. One exploded by the pier injuring eight people and causing the first loss of life. From then on we often saw a Blackburn Skua towing a target for firing practice for the guns along the seafront and Labrador. The raid that demolished part of Powderham Terrace was probably intended for Morgan Giles shipyard where I later learned my trade as a boat builder. Much debris was showered on the workshops but production carried on as usual.

My father, badly disabled as a result of the first war, joined Shaldon Home Guard and spent his duty time in the Guard Room in Fore St. We lived at Garston, backing on to farm buildings and a yard belonging to Frank Wood. I was hanging over our fence watching the cows coming in for milking one afternoon when a plane flew very low over our house. I immediately turned and ran in to scramble into the Morrison shelter that doubled as our dining room table. In the time it had taken me to reach the shelter, the plane had dropped a bomb smack in the middle of the bowling green. It bounced over our house and all the others in its path and exploded a quarter of a mile away in the allotments beside the Torquay Rd, just below The Hamiltons. It left a very large crater. It was probably the luckiest day of my life since a large piece of shrapnel from that bomb was found embedded in our back door, through which I had run only seconds before the explosion. I managed to pick up the flights from the bomb, only to have them taken from me by some spoilsport adult. Boys treasured souvenirs of war and I had collected several live shells from the guns on Shaldon Bridge and a mortar bomb from the assault course at Labrador, also a lump of SMS high explosive, about a pound and a half in weight from the beach. My father, in his wisdom, relieved me of that bit of ordnance just as I was about to find out if it would burn!

The village had two other raids, both at night. Two bombs were dropped by the river, one demolishing half of Teign House Hotel next to St Peter's Church and the other exploding harmlessly on the beach. The third raid was when a stray bomber dropped a crate of incendiary bombs into marshy ground belonging to the Carters of Higher Ringmore. The next day, some village boys were found to be in possession of a few of these unexploded bombs which were only about 12 inches in length and easy to conceal under a coat. The local constabulary were quick to confiscate these trophies, much to the disgust of the boys! On one occasion several of us boys had a competition to see if live bullets would explode if they were placed on a rock and hit with the back of an axe. They do. The result was many bleeding cuts to the hands and legs to say nothing of the ringing in our ears and a shattered axe.....all good fun!

After the arrival of the Americans, we saw a lot more activity around the harbour and the towns and villages. Landing craft were being built ready for the invasion of Europe and a series of concrete slipways were installed on the car park area in front of the Lifeboat Station. I remember watching Americans training in the 2-man midget submarines, sometimes called "Human Torpedoes". They were not short of money, food, cigarettes or chewing gum and were very generous. I was passing the cookhouse one day when a cook asked if I would like some peaches. He filled a large jam tin and I shared it with two pals on our way home. When I told my father he remarked that he and my brothers would have enjoyed a few of them. My feeling of guilt has lasted to this day.

Two of my brothers had left home by the middle of the war. The eldest to work in an aircraft factory at Bristol and the other joined the training ship Mercury on the Hamble in preparation for HMS Norfolk during the final stages of the war.

Despite his disability, father made sure that his boys spent very little of their school holidays in town and took us out to Labrador camping on the cliffs and beach. Much of the area was mined but the coastguard, Frank Thomas made sure that we stayed in safe areas. From our safe lookout at "Cherry Red" as we called it, we witnessed the air raid on St Marychurch when 21 children were killed at Sunday School. We also saw a large raid on Exmouth, dog fights out over the channel and the rescue of the crew by men in small boats when a Dutch coaster was on fire, just off Hope's Nose. German fighter-bombers flew very close to the cliff face to avoid cliff top guns and we saw the pilots quite clearly. We found a quantity of US military equipment including tins of emergency rations on the beach and enjoyed the biscuits, chocolate and glucose sweets. Later, I understood that this gift of goodies came from the unfortunate incident when 700 American servicemen perished a few miles from here in Lyme Bay when German E-Boats attacked their convoy of landing craft. We watched our American friends leave our shores on their way to the hell of the D-Day landings and saw them come back after being attacked in the channel. A lot of surplus equipment, including live ammunition, was left behind as the Americans vacated seafront hotels at Teignmouth. Those days from 1939-45

Steps in the cliff at Labrador

were memorable. Looking back, I suppose they were dangerous and things could have turned out so differently if Hitler had made fewer mistakes and the Allies had not had some lucky breaks. I tell my grandchildren that they live in more dangerous times now than we lived in....we only had a world war to threaten us.

**Powderham Terrace after raid on
10th January 1943**

Shaldon in Wartime by Trevor Jackson

Being one of six young boys
We never had that many toys
At the time there was a war on
Because of Hitler - that old moron!
We teased our leaders for some fun
Knocked their doors then off would run
Our parents would be very peeved
When they found out how we mischieved!
Mr Dunn who made the bread
And made sure that we were fed
Mr Irish at the dairy
Which was always clean and airy.
Then of course, there were the Sharlands
An ancient family of old ship hands
Henry, Manuel, George and Walter
All lived with Maud who was their sister.
Mr Denner was the grocer
Mr Cribble sold us papers
Mr Wood supplied the meat
And Salter's fish was such a treat.
Owing to the nightly black-out
Outdoor play was quite a wash-out
Winter nights were spent indoors
Playing games and banging doors.
It never came to rape and pillage
In the old days in our village.
The use of drugs it was unheard
Fresh air and sunshine were preferred.
Our names were not as we were christened
If they were used - no-one listened
Buster Ingram, Nobby Hook,
Buckle Cann and good old Smut
Snacker, Bumpy and Perp Drew
Just to name a very few.
Guffy Jackson, Giddy Thomas, Shrimpy Mole and old Flo Cann
Charlie Soper on the ferry,
Prudence always wore a beret.
Summer evenings oars would swish
When we had free fights with jelly fish.
Salty cockles for the taking

They just took a bit of raking
When the weather was hot and sweaty
We took a dive off Dolly's jetty.
Naval guns down at the Ness
When they were fired there was no rest
Yanks and tanks and landing craft
They trained here for the last great draft.
As we played the war went on
Over our roof bounced one big bomb
It hit the Green then took re-flight
But damage done was very slight.
When not at school throughout the war
We used to camp at Labrador
The super place to which we fled
Was named by father "Cherry Red".
We still return to that great place.
When our tired old bones can take the pace
We watched the air raids round about
From the mound we called out Lookout.
We never came to any harm
Perhaps we had a lucky charm
At times we got a little mucky
Many kids weren't half as lucky.
When the children of today
Go out into the streets to play
They sadly need far more protection
Then we did when there was a war on.

Mavis Keitch nee Symon

I was born in Teignmouth in 1933 and lived at Northam, 43 Higher Brimley. I was in Brook Hill School when it was bombed, upstairs in Mrs Stone's class. She was a large lady and was wearing a purple costume on the day of the bombing. The classroom had a screen that could be closed to make two rooms but on this day it was open. The blast of the bombs shunted the desks along to one end. We were sheltering underneath our desks and the glass cases of stuffed birds were smashed and feathers went everywhere. As I "came to" Mrs Stone was about to disappear out of the classroom and I shouted to her to wait for me. Sheila Rew who lived a few doors away sometimes came to play in our garden where we had made a seesaw from a plank. Suddenly, a black German plane came hedge-hopping over the gardens but there had been no siren warning. It was low enough for us to see the pilot's face. He began to machine-gun us but the sheets hanging on the line gave us some protection. We fled down the garden, jumping from the top of four steps across a narrow yard and straight through the back door - luckily wide open. Mother rushed from the kitchen as we fell through the doorway. She was a customer of Armstead's Dairy in Brook Hill and helped there by doing the washing when baby Noel arrived. I always visited the dairy on trips home in the 1960s. There is a family connection through my aunt to the Hamlyns who were killed in the air raid on Bitton Avenue in July '42. Marjorie Hamlyn and I had danced round the maypole together at school. This newspaper cutting is illuminating.

Enemy raiders flying low machine-gunned and bombed a southwest town on Wednesday afternoon. It was of the hit-and-run order and some people, including elderly persons were killed in addition to other casualties. Children were about to leave school when the planes arrived, but were kept under shelter by the teachers. A couple of bombs fell in a narrow thoroughfare resulting in many working-class houses being destroyed or badly damaged. Another wiped out a large boarding house, which was unoccupied at the time. Through a bomb exploding in a residential area, considerable damage was done to property and to a church. Several people had miraculous escapes, a bullet from a machine gun lodging in a boy's overcoat, which he was carrying on his arm. Glass from houses and business establishments flew in all directions. The work of clearing the debris was carried out with all possible speed, members of the forces giving ready and valuable assistance.

Ian Kilpatrick, son of Dr Ross Kilpatrick on the promenade late 1930s
Esplanade and Berkeley Hotels in background were destroyed by enemy action September 1942

Diane Kitcher nee Hooper

I was born in Teignmouth in 1933 and lived at 17 Somerset Place with my parents William and Edith, brothers Derek and Barry and grandparents Charles and Emma Boyne. Dad, a sergeant in the Territorial Army Devonshire Regiment was called up immediately war broke out. Soon afterwards we were issued with gas masks checked at school to see that they worked properly. Paper was placed underneath the nozzle then we took a breath and if the paper stuck to the nozzle it was working OK. Life seemed to continue much as usual, going to school and out to play but everywhere you went you had to take your gas mask. When the war started we didn't have a shelter so we used the cupboard under the stairs, strengthened by Durham Light Infantrymen, former miners, stationed in the former Conservative Club next door. The first time I heard bombs dropping was late at night. German planes flew over us on their way to bomb towns such as Plymouth and any bombs left over were dropped on Teignmouth to make their planes lighter for the journey home when their fuel was getting low. I attended Brook Hill Primary School, a large three storey building on the top of a small hill surrounded by houses. When an air raid started, the drill was to get down under the desks with our arms over our heads. The school day ended when the bell was rung at 4pm and hundreds of children would stream out of their classrooms, down the stairs and into the playground. One day, for some unknown reason (Uncle Fred was convinced it was the hand of God) the bell was late and we were still sitting at our desks when a raid started. I heard the breaking of glass in the window to my left and saw bullets fly across the classroom to a screen and holes appearing in it. It was a terrible noise as bombs were dropped on either side of the school. I was on my knees under the desk, second from the back. Everyone was screaming and crying, including me. Plaster and glass was falling all around us and the floor was shaking. When the raid was over, I found myself at the front of the class. As news got out that the school had been bombed, parents were racing to collect their children. Mother found my brother Derek but imagine her horror when she could not find me. A friend of hers found me wandering about and had taken me home covered from head to foot in plaster dust and blood on my legs from crawling through broken glass. Only after becoming a parent myself did I realize what she suffered, not knowing if I was dead or alive.

Methodist Church and Lyceum Cinema, Somerset Place

We went to the Gospel Hall every week and once, because we were being naughty, mother decided to set out early. We crossed the railway bridge and mother left us at Sunday School. A raid began and we lay on the floor with terrible sounds all around, bombs exploding and children screaming. It seemed as if the hand of God was on us again because if we had left home at the normal time, we would have been walking up the street during the bombing. Grandfather often stood at the front door listening to the drone of enemy planes overheard until the night the hospital was bombed and the blast blew him along the passage. The fright he got stopped him doing it again! Our shelter was in the back room of the house and I would never get out of bed if the siren sounded so I was made to sleep in the shelter instead of my bed. When we were playing rounders in Stanley St, a plane firing a machine gun came towards us so we ran into the nearest house and got under the table. A bomb fell on the Town Hall, smashing all the windows in our house. Mother and grandmother were outside sweeping up the glass when an Air Raid warden yelled at them " Get indoors you stupid women, there's an unexploded bomb across the road". We had to evacuate the area overnight whilst the bomb was diffused and our windows repaired. We spent two magical weeks on a farm near where my father was stationed at East Prawle. Another raid took place on a lovely summer evening when Dad and Granddad had taken us over to Salty in a boat and we heard the sound of engines. A dark plane came in over the mouth of the river and dropped two bombs. One of the houses in Bitton Avenue shattered into the air. Dad threw us into the bottom of the boat and covered us with his body to protect us from the debris falling all around. Granddad was standing up in the boat, shaking his fist and swearing at the plane! I remember seeing the sky above Shaldon glowing bright red as Plymouth burned. I never recall being cold or hungry and my childhood was very happy despite the fact that the war years were often frightening.

Doris Lane nee Gallin

My most vivid memory is of looking out of the window of the Post Office flat and seeing my mother running like mad down the bowling green to get my brother who was playing on the Den. A skit-skat of bullets followed her. My brother hid in the ladies toilet of the clubhouse and, not wanting to be left in the flat on my own, I made my way down to the switch room of the Telephone Exchange only to find four bottoms facing me! The switchboard girls had all got their heads under a very large table. I guess they thought that if their heads were safe - they were!

Post Office, Den Rd 1930s

Derek Ledger

I was born in Coombe Park Road in 1934. When bombs fell near Brook Hill School, I was in Miss Short's classroom, sheltering under a desk. Most of us had minor cuts from broken window glass and when things died down, we were told to go to the shelter. However, I went to retrieve my "new" raincoat (probably from a Jumble Sale) from the cloakroom. It had gone. Then I couldn't find the shelter so decided to run home to Coombe Park Rd, about a mile away. I went out into Brook St, turned left towards Fore St and was confronted by smoking ruins on both sides of the road. I jumped over the debris, dodging several men who tried to stop me and ran along Bitton St. I turned into Coombe Rd and found my relieved mother racing to meet me. I had another close shave in St James Parish Hall when a bomb dropped close by on The Groves. The morning after the whistling bombs fell in fields near Headway Cross (known to us as Heddy Cross) I woke up on the settee downstairs. My brother had carried me down and I had slept through it all. I remember the cannon shell near the clock in the Carlton Cinema. I sometimes think I was inside at the time but cannot swear to it as memory can play tricks but the hole remained for years. We kids were encouraged to stay out in the fields during air raids as it was thought to be safer. We witnessed several dogfights overhead and often saw planes doing a victory roll.

Home Guard training on Haldon
John's father, Hedley Mardon 2nd R

John Hedley Mardon

John was born in Boscawen Place in 1925 and became a carpenter with Young the Builder, transferring into Morgan Giles shipyard on a reserved occupation.
His widow Noreen nee Aggett has retained numerous documents including this certificate.

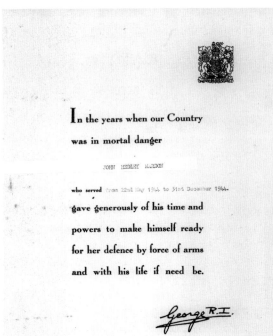

In the years when our Country was in mortal danger

JOHN HEDLEY MARDON

who served from 22nd May 1944 to 31st December 1944 gave generously of his time and powers to make himself ready for her defence by force of arms and with his life if need be.

George R.I.

THE HOME GUARD

Kathleen Mary Marinkovic nee Barge

Born 1910 in Plymouth, Kitty moved to Teignmouth in 1936, working as a dispenser for Maunder the Chemist in Somerset Place. She sang in the choir of the Methodist Church and was a member of the Repertory Company, Camera Club & Art Society. She is pictured in the garden of her home at Warberry in Third Drive off Landscore Rd. The year is 1941 and she wears a new ARP uniform ready for duty at the Report Centre. Her niece, Margaret Vosper, now cherishes a small printed card, saved by Kitty from wartime.

Give to our Leaders - Wisdom
Give to our men - Courage and Endurance
Give to me - Faith
Give to the Allies - Victory

Jim Matthews

As a lad in wartime, Jim was at Ern Roper's hut down near the Point. Also gathered there were some true river beach die-hards, Bill and Harry Trout, Ern Nathan and Pixie Matthews. Bill Trout looks up river and says, "Here come a couple of Hurricanes". The men crowd into the doorway to watch the aircraft believing them to be British. To their surprise, the aircraft suddenly opened up canon shellfire. It was an enemy plane! All the men tipped "base over apex" backwards into the hut!

On another occasion, Jim who had been injured by shrapnel during Teignmouth's first raid in July 1940 was between the Point car park and the beach when he saw two Focke Wulfs 190s flying down river. He watched as they went out over the sea, followed the coast and shot up a train near Dawlish Warren. Jim and Jack Hook, working boats out in local waters in the 1960s, located a half-loaded magazine of 20mm shells and the wing of a FW190. The wing is still buried deep in the sands of Teignmouth and might, one day, be uncovered by accident or design.

Overview of river beach and Morgan Giles shipyard

PO Ernest Menghini

Born in Landscore Rd in 1918, Ernest became a Boy Seaman at the age of 18. Hard discipline was the order of the day during training at St Vincent, Gosport and on his first ship, HMS Devonshire. In 1939 he joined HMS Stronghold as a Petty Officer and took passage for Singapore to teach the Malays to mine sweep. This duty lasted 3 years and his family had almost given up hope of Ernest as there had been no contact but he returned home on HMS Dauntless in 1942. After marrying Rita Boyne he set off almost at once for the war in North Africa on HMS Tynedale. They chased submarines and fortunately for Ernest, he left the ship before she was sunk. During D-Day training off Salcombe, the crew of LST 180 narrowly missed a disastrous situation when a converted cross channel ferry rammed it. The LST left from Southampton and arrived at Arromanches at 06.30 on 6th June 1944, discharging equipment as hostilities raged all around. Bombardment from ships, air attack and fire from snipers created a hellish situation. A wire had snared the LST's screw, so in the midst of all the hostilities, engineers fought to solve the problem with cutting gear and blowtorches. Despite the confusion, Ernest decided that the ship's nanny goat Angus needed fresh herbage and attached her to a length of rope to walk her over the bridgehead ... the crew laughed their heads off!

LST 180 made repeated trips between Normandy and Southampton, carrying the injured back and returning with more equipment. It was fitted up as a hospital ship with 4 operating tables and bunks in the tank space. Lord Lovatt was brought aboard, close to death and survived. After the injured were embarked, the Skipper received a signal to bury the dead at 11 am. Most were Canadian and identity discs were gathered from the bodies, pitifully wrapped in blankets. As Chief Roman Catholic aboard, Ernest was told to take care of the religious part. The Prayer Book issued to him in 1936 provided the spiritual source for the poor souls crossing the bar. "Those bodies could have been landed at Southampton and returned home. It was harsh and even after all these years, it still sticks in my gullet." Reflecting on the war and 22+ years service in the Royal Navy followed by 20 years as Teignmouth's Harbour Master, Ernest says, " I was lucky - never got wounded - never even got my feet wet! The Good Lord has been a shining star for me."

**Petty Officer Menghini on an Indian Charger
at Mhow Rest Camp January 1946**

Francis Charles Morgan-Giles OBE MINA 1883-1964

Francis served in RNVR throughout World War 1. In 1920, he bought the shipyard in Teignmouth and earned an enviable reputation building first-class racing and cruising yachts of all descriptions. It was expanded to meet Admiralty demands during the second war and built over 100 vessels from small craft to powerful MTBs and minesweepers. Francis was awarded an OBE and made an honorary Liveryman of the Worshipful Company of Shipwrights and Freeman of the City of London.

Sir Morgan Charles Morgan-Giles Rear Admiral

S.N.O at Vis 1944

Morgan, born in 1914, the first son in the family of five, became a Naval Officer. In the first winter of the war he was escorting Atlantic Convoys in HMS Emerald and was involved in the Norwegian Campaign. From December 1940 until 1944, he was continuously in the Mediterranean and took part in the Battle of Oran. Morgan was minesweeping in the Suez Canal and served in the Tobruk garrison throughout most of the siege. During the "Invasion Era" he took part in an abortive Fire ship Operation off the French Coast. After some months in Malta and Algiers he was sent to the Italian East Coast port of Bari. In late 1943 when Churchill took the strategic decision to support Tito's Partisan Resistance, Morgan organized "gun running" operations to the Dalmatian Coast of Yugoslavia. The following year, he was in charge of all RN operations from the island of Vis in the Yugoslavian Islands. These included landings with Army units, Royal Marine Commandos and Fitzroy Maclean's military and political mission to Tito.

The Luftwaffe attacked the port of Bari when it was crowded with two large shipping convoys on 2nd December 1943. Morgan, enjoying a drink in a bar when the raid began, dashed down to Navy House on his motorbike. Orders had been given to clear the harbour where the first stricken ship had filled the harbour with oil. The second, an ammunition ship, blew up sending burning wreckage all over the harbour and setting many other ships on fire. Mustard gas shells were scattered on top of the oil floating all around the harbour. Morgan was uninjured after being blown the length of the deck of HMS Zetland. He set about carrying out orders to remove disabled ships and took the Captain's motorboat over to a large American merchant ship, Lyman Abbott, lying at anchor close by. He clambered aboard as it lay in darkness, without power or crew left alive. Amidst dreadful confusion and increasing fires, Morgan and two others used a scuttling charge to sever the anchor chain, enabling a tug to tow her clear. Seventeen ships were sunk and 1000 men killed in Bari's small harbour that night.

From early 1945 until the end of the Japanese war he was employed with Combined Operations in the Far East. In 1964, he was elected Conservative MP for Winchester and spent 15 years in Parliament. Morgan was instrumental in saving HMS Belfast, which he had re-commissioned at Singapore in 1961, as a museum ship on the Thames.

Michael Alfred Lonsdale Morgan-Giles Captain RE

Port Operations Venice 1945

After a year's service with the Royal Fleet Auxiliary, Michael was commissioned into the Royal Engineers in 1942. He was posted to the Mediterranean to take charge of a Port Operating Company RE in North Africa, Sicily and Italy. Towards the end of the conflict, he was put in charge of Port Operations at Venice. In later years, he ran the shipyard, was Chairman of Teignmouth Harbour Commission and a JP. Michael was Chairman of Teignmouth Urban District Council 1964/5 and died in 1980.

Hebe Constance Morgan-Giles

ATS Officer 1944

At the outset of war Hebe, housekeeping for her father, was suddenly required to drive him all over Britain in connection with the numerous craft for the Admiralty under construction in his shipyard. She joined Shaldon Home Guard under Major Bigg-Wither. On a trip to Plymouth, Hebe and her father found the entire timber yard on fire after a bombing raid the previous night. In 1942, she joined the ATS and served in Heavy Anti-Aircraft batteries. Two years later she was commissioned into the ATS where she drove Generals and Senior Officers on official duties right round the clock.

Commander Christopher Paul Morgan-Giles

Christopher, the fourth of five children, was born in 1922 at the family home Cliffside, Shaldon. He was 17 when the war began and joined the Royal Navy serving as a Lieutenant, mostly at sea in the South Atlantic and Mediterranean. He had a very active time, gaining four stars and two medals. Christopher's reputation as a gifted raconteur is known far and wide and here is one of his best.

"We were on escort duty in HMS Birmingham trying to shepherd a Cape convoy of slow and ancient merchant ships through a pack of 16 U-Boats in the Bay of Biscay. Our Walrus flying boat took off with Pilot and Observer on anti-submarine patrol and was never seen again. When we reached Freetown over a week later, we took the first opportunity to hold a memorial service for our gallant aviators. A tiny speck on the horizon, which grew larger and larger and turned out to be a native fishing canoe containing our aircrew, emaciated and blackened by the sun, interrupted the service. The only fisherman who had not hurriedly absconded in fear when they let off their distress flares as the aircraft sank, and who now produced them just in time for their own memorial service had rescued them! Naturally we all made a great fuss of the brave black fisherman, presented him with £25 from the ship's fund, which would have got him a new canoe, new house and a new wife if he wanted them. I prepared an elaborate certificate testifying to his courageous deed and in my best colonial tone said loudly "What is your name?" Upon which he drew himself up to his full enormous height, grinned broadly and in ringing tones cried "Sir Henry Newbolt!" which, of course, was immediately inscribed on his certificate!

Robin Fulke Morgan-Giles

The youngest family member ran away from school at the age of 16 to join up. When all the windows at the shipyard were blown out during the raid in January '43, Robin was stationed at the entrance to protect the vast amount of valuable equipment that had been blown out into the road. He was signed in as a Third officer in the Merchant Navy and at one time, put in charge of the engines of a large target towing motor launch at Plymouth.

Hugh Nettleton

I was born in 1931 and attended Thornpark School on the upper side of Coombe Vale Rd close to the junction with Landscore Rd. Run by Miss West and Miss Elsie, both elderly ladies with Miss Lard putting in an occasional appearance at the piano. It catered for 30-40 children including the Mills twins Pat and Joan who lived further along the road and Diana Good of Hobarts in Wellington St. The schoolroom was on the main floor as you entered from the road. The dining room downstairs opened onto a garden that sloped away from the house and many large bushes marked its perimeter. The school was partly demolished during a half term break in November 1942 and the site is now occupied by Grendon Flats.

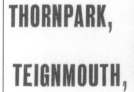

THORNPARK, TEIGNMOUTH, Situate in the Coombe Vale,

I was a patient in Teignmouth Hospital only 5 days before it was bombed in 1941. In July 1942 a friend and I were on the beach by the Point car park when two planes came in over the Ness. An adult told us to run and lie down at the bottom of the sea wall. Whether they were testing their guns or firing at us I shall never know but shells hit the wall and beach as we lay there. I left my sandals on the beach but ran home with my jar of crabs! The following month, just as we were sitting down to tea at home in the Devon Arms in Northumberland Place, bombs were dropped on the Market & Town Hall opposite. All our windows were blown out, doors blown off their hinges and some ceilings came down, including the kitchen where we sat. My first encounter with war injuries was seeing the fireman who had been killed in the explosion. An unexploded bomb fell diagonally into Brunswick Printing Works and ended up in the yard of Davies Café, opening on to Brunswick St. We were evacuated to Pittaway's on the corner of Ivy Lane. Dad went back home with our red setter Judy to keep an eye on our home that was now open to all-comers. Once the debris from the Town Hall was cleared, people prised up the parquet flooring blocks to use as fuel. They burned well since they had been laid in bitumen.

My birthday on Sunday 10th January 1943 coincided with the town's worst raid. We were sitting down to a late lunch of stuffed sheep's hearts when we heard bombs drop nearby. Lunch was forgotten as we all went down by the Marina Hotel in Powderham Terrace. I have a vivid memory of people coming out of their houses with smoke billowing out behind them. I looked up and saw that a mattress had draped itself neatly over the chimney of the houses next to Morgan Giles shipyard. I have lived in New Zealand for many years but hope to re-visit home.

Flooding in Northumberland Place 1930s.
Mrs Nettleton outside the Devon Arms

NEWSPAPERS

Teignmouth Post of 1940

July Petty Sessions. A Dawlish man was summonsed for driving a car, which did not have its bumpers, painted with white paint or other white material. Fined £1.

An occupant of Bickford Lane was fined ten shillings for not observing Blackout regulations. Police had obtained a 16-foot ladder to observe her extension with four unscreened lights.

Riviera Cinema

Of all the films in which Fred Astaire and Ginger Rogers have co-starred perhaps the most popular and most memorable was "Follow the Fleet" and it is for this reason that this grand musical show has been revived and will be presented...next week.

The Pier

Manager J.J. Angliss announced... Still Carrying On...the Management regrets the Dances have had to be cancelled but hopes to be able to obtain another hall shortly.

Den Pavilion

Owing to existing circumstances, Mr A'Dell has decided to close down for the present after the performance on Saturday night next. Should the times require a resumption of "live" entertainment, arrangements will be made for a re-opening for which due notice will be given.

Millbay Cleaners

Wrong again Lord Haw Haw! Rumour has it that Lord Haw Haw has inferred that clothes will be so scarce in England that we shall have nothing to wear. Rubbish! Apparently he has overlooked Millbay Special Cleaning service which will repeatedly lengthen the life and restore the original appearance of the oldest and shabbiest garment.

Food Control Committee

EW Parsons, Chairman of Teignmouth Food Control Committee has set up an office for the "Cheap Milk Scheme".

TH Aggett is Milk Officer and SH Ware is Hon Secretary dealing with surplus fruit disposal. Special permits are issued to farmers enabling them to get sugar for drinks for casual workers and on special occasions such as harvest time. Some 25 honorary workers assist with issuing the second series of ration books – 9737 for adults and 489 for children.

NEWSPAPERS

Save Old Ration Books!

Some 50 million out of date Ration Books nationwide contained pages of coupons included for use in an emergency. The Ministry of Food urge the public to include these pages with other paper going to local salvage depots. The Ministry itself saved seven square miles of paper by gluing together the pages of new Ration Books so they could be sent through the post without using envelopes.

Grow More Food!

The Council received a letter from the National Allotments Society urging that, in view of the great need for increased home food production, it is vitally necessary that a supreme effort should be made to produce more food from allotments and gardens this season. Growers who have produced in excess of their requirements are asked not to waste it but to make it available for disposal, either by sale or in the form of gifts to the Hospital or to poor people. We cannot afford to waste anything.

The Ministry of Home Security

700,000 copies of a 3d pamphlet "Your home as an air raid shelter" were sold. Another pamphlet "Air Raids: What you must know: What you must do" is a potted ARP course for the general public. It deals with protection against bombs, behaviour during and after a raid, incendiary bombs and war gasses.

Borrowed Children

A booklet suggesting remedies to the problems attached to evacuated children. It is a fascinating record, intimate and actual, of dozens of cases of what happened in those first extraordinary few days in September 1939 and in the months that followed.

Radio News

The broadcast from Hamburg on Saturday night announced that Sdr Ldr Brian Paddon of Clifton, Teignmouth who was shot down near Abbeville on June 26th is a prisoner of war.

W.V.S for Aluminium Appeal.

Cllr Kate Anson Cartwright promises "Your pots and pans will be turned into Spitfires, Hurricans, Blenheims and Wellingtons". Gather pots, pans, vacuum cleaners, hat pegs, coat hangers, shoe trees, bathroom fittings, household ornaments, cigarette boxes, or any other articles made wholly or in part from aluminium and deliver them to Mr Kingdon at Regent St.

Albert Penwill

As an employee of GWR, known as God's Wonderful Railway, I was required to join their Local Defence Unit. We had to patrol the line between Shaldon Bridge and Parson & Clerk Rocks and one dark, wet and windy night, George Lang and I were near the tunnel when we heard the crunch of boots on ballast. "Leave this to me" said George "Halt! Who goes there?" Silence, except for the howling wind. The footsteps began again so George repeated his challenge. Still silence, so we continued to walk along the line. Once again, the footsteps started. "Halt or I'll fire!" shouted George and a voice from the darkness asked "Who are you?" George replied "Home Guard - who are you?" Back came the reply "I'm the Coastguard!" The railway line was out of bounds to unauthorized persons, including Coastguards, and he should have been on the sea wall but found it more sheltered walking inside the boundary wall.

Dorcas Porter nee Stowers

I was born at Trull in Somerset and our family moved to Teignmouth when I was 3 months old. When war broke out I was 13 and remember helping at the WVS Canteen in the hall of Our Lady & St Patrick's Church on Dawlish Rd, often visited by American troops. We looked forward to our once a week get-together at Burlington House in Mere Lane to knit mittens, scarves and balaclavas for servicemen, as well as mending

Local children found beach barricades were fun

their damaged clothing and underclothes. Miss Best, the Infant teacher at Brook Hill School, was one of the mending party and embroidered a beautiful red rose on a pair of underpants scheduled to be returned to a serviceman! We often wrote little notes and tucked them in to give a word of encouragement to the recipient. Sometimes, men of the Parachute Regiment billeted in town visited us and we had a good laugh together. Grammar School Master Harold Wheeler led groups up Breakneck Hill to Furze Copse to collect sacks of fir cones. They were sent away but I never discovered what they were used for. It was a real highlight to watch the Yanks play baseball matches on the Den. Rastus, one of the servicemen always played with a cigar in his mouth and when it was his turn to bat, he threw it to the ground, raced round the circuit, retrieved the cigar and carried on with his smoke! Wives and mothers had a lot to put up with and suffered such anxiety about their husbands and sons away at war. It was our job at home to boost morale and keep cheerful. Nobody seemed to grumble at each other then. It wasn't all doom and gloom…the war brought many jolly times.

CPO Reginald Robins

Reg was born in Saxe St in 1921. At the age of 14 he became an apprentice shipwright at Morgan Giles shipyard. Call Up was twice deferred but he eventually went into the Navy. He adored the sea but suffered terrible seasickness. Little is known about Reg's service but became a Chief Petty officer in the Royal Navy serving on Wayland and was stationed at Mombasa for a while. His ship crossed the Equator in 1943 and a linen certificate recording that crossing is a treasured reminder. He met Pat from the Midlands and moved there to live after their marriage in 1946. It proved to be too far from his beloved sea so they returned to Teignmouth and Reg went back to work as a shipwright at Morgan Giles. He died in 1995 and is remembered affectionately as a man full of fun by all who knew him.

Leading Shipwright Ronald John Rodwell

Born in the Mission to Seamen at 26 Teign St in 1924 where his parents were stewards, Ron remembers religious services each Sunday night led by Preacher Joe Dunning, whose name lives on at Dunning's Walk. Numerous seafarers came in search of a bath and place to rest their head, and one officer was destined to help Ron at the outset of his war service. Schooling at Brook Hill began at the age of 3 years. Each afternoon, the infants climbed on their classroom tables and took a nap. At 13, Ron began an apprenticeship as a boat builder with Morgan Giles. Because he was able to swim, Foreman Tom Vincent took him sailing in 16-foot Dart 1 class yachts entering all the Regattas along the South Devon Coast. Ron volunteered for the Royal Navy and went to Glenholt on Dartmoor's western edge for basic training. The Master of Arms took one look at him and said " Rodwell – are you from Teignmouth?" He remembered the Rodwell's kindness at the Mission so he gave Ron the task of keeping his cabin clean and sharing supper each evening. This compared very favourably to other tasks!

Ron joined the Coastal Forces, trained at Largs near Port Glasgow on the Clyde and served aboard MTBs. The skills of a shipmate who doctored rail tickets by bleaching and re-writing with swan ink, allowed him to get home to Teignmouth for a long weekend leave when he did not have the price of the fare. In the build up to the Invasion, Ron was transferred to Combined Operations based near Chichester where he tasted a turkey dinner for the first time. During the Normandy landings, Damage Control was his responsibility whilst he helped to ferry tanks and troops from the LCT to various beaches then return to the Depot ship for another batch. He transferred to HMS Unicorn, an Aircraft Carrier patrolling the British coast. When his wife Joyce fell seriously ill, he was given a Compassionate Draft to Devonport. In later years, Ron and Joyce developed a great interest in Elkhounds, keeping several and showing them all over the country.

Janet Roper

with sister Joan (R) serving in WRNS

In 1940 Janet was 4 years old when she stood with her mother and a cluster of locals at the Point as a convoy of 15 to 20 local boats headed over the bar for Dunkirk. Her father Ernest was on his clinker-built boat Sapphire that he worked as a pleasure boat until it was requisitioned. Jack Broom and Jack Hitchcock were part of the convoy. Having reached the Dorset coast, Sapphire was ordered to turn back. The Ropers lived in Teign View Place where all residents had to get used to being barred from the beach beyond their front doors due to anti-invasion measures installed when it was believed that England was in serious danger of being over-run by the enemy. A barricade of criss-crossed scaffolding and barbed wire stretched right around Teignmouth's waterside. Janet knew she was not allowed to go on the beach but did not understand why because her parents played the situation down and tried to live as normal a life as possible. She was enjoying an ice cream in Forte's café at the Triangle when the first raid occurred on the seafront. The windows shattered and she was upset not to be able to finish the treat because of the glass now embedded in it. In September 1942, the Ropers and their friend Elsie Pritchard were at the Point when planes dropped bombs on the town. Ernest realized they had fallen in the area of the school and raced across to find Janet. When the raid began, she was just leaving the building and had been pushed into the shelter in the playground. A water pipe had been damaged and Shute Hill looked surreal awash with water, stained deep red by soil. Elsie's mother had been killed in her house next to the Co-op on Higher Brook St. Ernest took Janet home and broke the sad news to Elsie and her daughter Margaret returning by train from her workplace in Torquay. Their home and all their belongings were gone so they moved in with the Ropers for a while and Margaret was given half Joan's clothes.

It was decided that the family should move to Scotland where Ern, stationed near Fort William served on Carlo, one of six ammunition ships on Loch Eil. Although they were frequently required to show their identity cards to Military Police, life in the highlands was like being in another world. Joan served with the WRNS for two years towards the end of the war and when she was stationed in barracks at Greenock, smuggled Janet aged 10 to stay with her in a nissen hut with bunk beds and a coal-burning stove. Joan and her colleagues secreted the stow-away during roll call and breakfast was smuggled to her each morning. If the Petty Officers in the adjacent cabin had any idea of her presence, they let it pass even though she ran the gauntlet by jumping noisily on the loose manhole cover on the way down the hill to ablutions! Joan was a sea-going Wren relaying messages

Ernest Roper (R) at Loch Eil near Fort William

to ships in the Clyde. A car took her to the quayside where she was met by a local trawler or drifter and conveyed to one of the ships before they sailed for wartime duties. Janet was lucky enough to visit an American ship and was showered with fruit and chocolate, such as she had never seen before. A close view of the great vessel Queen Elizabeth was also thrilling. Bus passengers in Greenock and Glasgow were expected to jump on and off whilst the bus was in motion and Janet's adventure ended after mis-timing her jump. She hit her head on the kerb and ended up in the barrack sickbay with concussion but this did not detract from the wonderful holiday shared with her adored sister.

James Skerrett

The 1995 Teignmouth Old Grammarians Association accorded top table to nine men and their wives, a group with a peculiar unity. The men were the last traceable members of the "Hostel Boys" who shared an existence at the former nurses' hostel. Those boys, and six others had roamed far and wide but regrouped for the 50th Anniversary of their arrival. The hostel in Mill Lane had not suffered as badly as the hospital, reduced to tumbled rubble by Hitler in 1941, and was refurbished by September 1945 ready for the 15 and their mentor, PI Instructor Gervase Jones. The immediate post-war years were difficult for all save spivs. Shortages of food, fuel and commodities of all sorts called for a continuation of the Dunkirk spirit long after VJ Day, but we were hardened to it.

Despite being a separate group we never felt that we were outsiders. Under Mr Silverston's leadership, the school, accustomed to accepting evacuees absorbed us without any apparent difficulty. The sporting abilities of many of the group gained them rapid entry into the world of football, cricket and athletic elite, while the sudden widening of choice of female company provided delights hitherto undreamt of. There was, of course, a downside. We washed dishes, made our own beds, polished our own floors, stoked the boilers and got our heads down to regular housework for an hour and a half each evening. Every Friday, two were detailed to collect the fish after school for the evening meal and they would lug the odorous load through the streets and up Mill Lane's gradient. Every Sunday, we attended church in the morning and wrote letters home in the evening after tea. "We played Newton Grammar yesterday and won 3-1. I got one and was crocked by their centre-half but I got him later"...jolly gripping stuff!

Life was never boring for we had no TV and found plenty of activities to fill our spare hours, making model aeroplanes and various woodcrafts as the Eisteddfod drew near. We used the hospital ruins for cricket practice; the empty corridor floors were super, if near lethal wickets. We devised homespun entertainments, played on the miniature billiard table with a bewildering list to windward. All this meant that attendance at school between 9 and 4 was just a tiresome interruption in the meaningful rhythm of life. Piano practice was relegated (sadly in retrospect) to the 20 minutes before setting off for the lesson with Mr Daulby Peake. When we went our separate ways, some to serve King and Country, others to university or college, we probably thought it was the end of our hostel experience. But our 1995 reunion to share anecdotes, confessions and repartee indicated that the experience had not been entirely without impact.

Eveline Sanders nee Stowers

After a probationary period at Dawlish Cottage Hospital in 1940, I became a Staff Nurse at the Royal Devon & Exeter Hospital. It was a very different world, very strict but with a strong sense of duty and service. Uniform was supplied except shoes and stockings. Rooms in the Nurses' Quarters were shared until I had my own as a State Registered Nurse. Wards doubled up to 40 beds each and two were set aside for the military. We cared for many casualties during the Exeter bombing, young and old, some from the outskirts and some from next door, The Valiant Soldier Inn, amongst the many buildings destroyed. The aftermath of D-Day was a hectic and sad time with our corridors full of injured military, many with shrapnel and bullet wounds, some still covered in sand. I carried on to become a Theatre Sister but it was the war years when nursing was so vital.

Pat Scagell

Pat was born in Custom House Hill in 1924. On his 18th birthday, Customs Officer, Mr Goldfinch accepted his request to join the Navy. His father, who had served in the Navy in the first war was very angry but soon Pat was off for training near Ipswich. He was sent first to Scotland and experienced numerous mines exploding all around in the Forth river where he served on an ML. "It made your teeth snap together hard, especially when 5 went off more or less at once". The bonus was that lots of cod surfaced and Pat used a gaff to hook them into the trawler. The water was white with sprats but he didn't bother with those! He spotted Ernie Chapman on another vessel on the Forth but was unable to hail him as they passed like two ships in the night. Pat went out to serve in Rangoon on RN harbour defence motor launches, taken as deck cargo on a liner. Coincidence dictated that Pat should meet another Teignmothian out in the east. He was at rest in a dark billet in Calcutta when the door opened and a man in uniform came in and looked around to see if there was a spare bed. All were occupied so he left without noticing Pat who followed him out. "Aren't you going to speak to me?" he asked of Jim Stowers, who was delighted to find a familiar face so many miles from home. Pat was a gunner on a cruiser when about 50 of them where sent to Mergui on Burma's coast to accept the surrender of 600 Japanese whose rifles were stacked up in pyramids of three. The most momentous sight was when Allied Prisoners were released at Rangoon. Many had lost a leg during the dreadful, prolonged

Pat and his mother, Emily in 1942

suffering but Pat will always remember the look of joy on their faces when they glimpsed the white ensign of his ship.

Pauline Seaton nee Rose

On the evening of Friday 1st September 1939, all the lights went out at the fair down on the Point after Hitler invaded Poland. Two days later when I returned home from singing in the choir of the Congregational Church, my parents said we were at war with Germany. Two girl evacuees from Acton came to us but most went back home during the "phoney war" before Dunkirk and Battle of Britain. The first raid on Teignmouth occurred on my 15th birthday. Grammar School pupils were instructed to seek shelter in the basement of the large houses in Landscore Rd. We carried gas masks everywhere and as a senior I was in charge of 2 first formers. Our newly built classrooms, Craft Block and Assembly Hall came in useful when pupils from the Haberdasher Aske's Schools had to be absorbed. During the summer of 1940, we took part in the Holiday Campaign. Every morning, weather permitting, we sat on the school lawn and knitted socks, gloves and balaclava helmets whilst the boys made splints for hospitals. Our Headmaster, Mr Silverston was asked to provide senior pupils to assist the Librarian Mr Short at the new library in Brunswick St and I helped there with my friend Margaret Tusler one night each week. In the Girls Training Corps we learned Morse code, Aircraft Recognition and First Aid. We prepared

refreshments for the boys in the school's ATC and marched proudly behind them in the parades during special weeks such as Salute the Soldiers, Warships, and Wings for Victory.

A national appeal was made for picture postcards of France after it fell to Germany in 1940. I sent in a collection received from my French pen pal. It would help detect the width of roads and other topographical details for the eventual invasion of Europe. They were returned to me after the war. After our first raid, the seafront was cordoned off and later we were not allowed on the beaches or sea wall. As each country fell and became our Allies, their National Anthem was played after Sunday Half Hour before the 9 o'clock News on the wireless. By 1941, I was working at Barclays Bank where women replaced the men who had been called up. When there was an alert, we had to take ledgers, cash and customers into the strong room. Many people left Teignmouth after the tip and run raids and for some months, it was a ghost town. You could walk through the centre and not see a soul.

I well remember the raid on 2nd September 1942. A teacher was about to open the big door of the school to let the children out, but heard something and quickly shut it again. What carnage there would have been from bombs, machine guns and cannon-fire? After a raid, you always made for home, not knowing what you would find. My mother was at home in 45 Higher Brook St with others who dashed in to take shelter and in the Bank, we realized bombs had dropped in my home area. One of my colleagues insisted on accompanying me. Crying children came running down Bickford Lane. My mother was looking for me but I did not recognize her at first as she was completely covered in yellow dust. Hilda Best the Infant teacher came to our house looking for her sister and mother. The Rescue Party searched for them all that night in the rubble of their home nearby and eventually recovered their bodies just outside their Morrison shelter.

Members of the Air Sea Rescue and Free French Navy including General de Gaulle's son and Humphrey Fisher, son of the Archbishop of London (Later Canterbury) were stationed here. One morning, I opened the Bank door and found myself surrounded by men of the US Navy wanting to exchange their money. Barclays was the official bank of the US Navy and we were kept very busy dealing with wires of flowers and "candy" to wives and sweethearts back home. A large house in Powderham Terrace became their Fleet Club. They collected money for charity at Baseball matches against what was left of our cricket team. The Den Pavilion became their mess room and local girls invited to dances there. In the Bank we listened to the broadcast about Victory in Europe and added patriotic decorations to the upper windows. I am glad to have lived my young years at this time because we learned to value life's simple pleasures even though we had so much to put up with including rationing of food and clothes – even lives. People were much kinder and helped each other without any thought of repayment. After being denied access to the beach and sea, what a pleasure it was to enjoy it again! That is why even now, just sitting quietly on the beach or at home is almost paradise.

Barclays Bank in Wellington St   May 1945

SNIPPETS

American servicemen: Billeted in seafront hotels, sent their shirts and uniforms to Teign St where Ivy May Robbins was renowned for first class ironing. Her sons delivered them back to the servicemen and their father, Edward George was a baker at the Co-op in Brook Hill.

Joan Atkinson: a greatly respected teacher of Physical Education and later Maths at Teignmouth Grammar School. During the war she became a National Savings fundraiser and gathered thousands of pounds by collecting all around the town. Her efforts were recognized and she was presented with a special certificate. Joan's mother took evacuees into her Barnsley Drive home and helped with salvage collecting and her sister Diana was nursing at Exmouth.

Joseph Charles Day: One of the well-known local fish merchants was in the Home Guard. After the raid on 10th January 1943, Joe helped clear up at Powderham Terrace. This involved moving a large amount of fallen masonry and heavy boulders. A few days later, he suffered a massive heart attack and died at the age of 49.

Brian Gilpin: Like many local lads, remembers being lucky enough to be given a meal by the Yanks using the Den Pavilion as a canteen. Hats "scrounged" from servicemen were greatly prized. Huge wooden crates were stacked up on the Den in the lead up to D Day. Once emptied, the boys made camp inside them.

The Rowdens 1930s: On nights when raids were expected, many people preferred to sleep out in the meadows of Eastcliff.

SNIPPETS

Nancy Hooper: All her long life remembered that the day after the Exeter Blitz in 1942, Park St, Teignmouth was covered with fragments of charred newsprint.

Rex Hitchcock: A Prisoner of War camp was set up in the fields near Inverteign Infant School. Most of the men were Italian and they carved beautiful toys and sold them for coppers. Every Sunday they were marched through the town to attend the service at the Catholic Church.

Morgan Edwards Family: Owned the Royal Hotel lived at Holcombe Down House at the top of Breakneck Hill. A daughter, Sue recalls two or three "fox holes" being dug outside their home, from where snipers could operate.

Doreen Penwill: Doreen's ordeal of being trapped under glass and masonry following an air raid was described in Teignmouth at War 1. Over the years several pieces of glass worked their way to the surface of her skin. Six decades after sustaining these injuries, a doctor removed another fragment of glass from Doreen's leg in February 2002

St Scholastica's Abbey: Nuns maintained Perpetual Prayer for the duration of war. David Robbins and his friend Donald Walters were altar boys.

Eric Searle: As a lad watched dive-bomb practice on large rafts belonging to Morgan Giles. There was a pole in the centre and on top, a big black ball. Bombs of white powder were fired at them and when the pilot scored a hit, the ball looked like a Christmas pudding! All the kids were taken to a hut on the Point to test out gas masks. "You went in one end and came out the other - it made your eyes water!"

Marie Stockman nee Squire: Her parents bought The Grotto opposite Eastcliff House on Dawlish road, later known as Overcliff (see photo page 137), soon after American troops vacated it in 1944. It had a tunnel beneath the road that was used as an air raid shelter and despite the poor state of the house, Mrs Squire chose it for that reason alone.

Fred Tooley: Recalls nissen huts close to where the Haldon Tea House once stood, accounting for the flatness of the location.

Rosa Victoria Turpin: A 55 year old lady from Shimpitt, Bishopsteignton, cycled into Teignmouth to buy a birthday present on the afternoon of 2nd September 1942. She was killed in the Brook Hill raid and laid to rest in Bishopsteignton cemetery.

Ethel Webber: In 1940 when invasion was feared, workers from Cox Marine engineering company of Dawlish St made weekly checks on the opening span of Shaldon Bridge. It could be a useful roadblock if the enemy invaded. The men involved were Claude Howard, Percy Scagell, Ern Wilcox and their boss Mr Cox. An interesting connection is that the author has lived in Percy Scagell's former home, Bridge View, since 1994.

Seaward side of Den Pavilion and barricades along the sea wall. Prior to bombing of Esplanade and Berkeley Hotels beyond

Eileen Stowers nee Westlake

It was late in 1943 that Eileen Westlake of Ivy Lane had an unusual and humorous experience. She worked in Teignmouth Post Office as a counter clerk and part time telephonist on night duty with the Fire Service HQ, having been refused permission to join the WRNS because of being in a reserved occupation. On the way to work early one morning, Eileen looked across Lower Den Rd and saw hundreds of men in an unfamiliar uniform sitting and lying across the pavement and grass beside heaps of equipment. She dashed back home in Ivy Lane and told her father Fred, a Morgan Giles shipwright that the Germans had landed! Cautiously, they returned to check the scene and were relieved to discover the United States Navy had arrived in Teignmouth and were resting on the Den, awaiting billets. Many of these same men took part in the Normandy landings on D-Day.

Shelter outside Lendrick School, close to where American troops were first seen on the Den

Edmund James Edworthy Stowers QPM

Jim's war service started with the RN and ended in the army with the 20th Indian Division

I served on a River Class Frigate, HMS Bann, direction finding on German submarine wireless transmissions in the Atlantic and the Sicily landing. Returning from North Africa with prisoners of war, the convoy was ironically bombed by dreaded Focke Wulf Condors. I was in the Far East for the next three years. After convoy escort duty, I trained in Ceylon to read Japanese wireless transmissions and was attached to Mobile Y (wireless intelligence) parties working near or behind Japanese lines.

Landing at Ramree, Burma, I lost my haversack and was kitted out in the stores at Akyab by John Ferris, whose home in Higher Brimley was only yards from mine in Heywoods Rd. I was amazed to meet him and other Teignmothians such as Eddie Stocker RAF in Bombay and Pat Scagell RN in Calcutta. I missed meeting Ron Cox by one day after he was evacuated from Burma with Jap gunshot wounds. Another memorable meeting was with my brother

The marriage of Jim Stowers and Eileen Westlake on 22nd November 1947 at St James Church

Edwin, an Admiralty Officer in Mauritius. I got permission to go ashore to meet him and it was twelve months to the day after saying our farewells on the platform of Teignmouth Railway station. VJ Day meant little to the 20th Indian Division, deep in the jungle where the Japanese were still holding out. I flew from Rangoon to Saigon in French Indo China. Out of the frying pan into the fire! Civil war broke out in opposition to the return of French rule and we had the difficult job of regaining law and order. At the Japanese SE Asia Wireless HQ near Saigon, I was Control Supervisor, protecting the camp against attack with five Gurkhas. I came home in 1946 and returned to the sea for a couple of years as Radio Officer MN. First on the Franconia evacuating the 6th Airborne Regiment from Palestine then troops from India. Defoe, my second ship worked South America and Australia. Happily marrying Eileen Westlake, I returned to civilian life.

Paul Tidball

I was born in 1937. My parents Fred and Jessie Tidball and my grandfather, George Bace and I lived in a house in Mulberry St. The first wartime incident I remember was an air raid at night when a bomb exploded in Bitton St and blew our kitchen window out. The next incident was by the far the most frightening. One summer evening, all the family were on the way to our allotment in St Mary's, opposite the Exeter Rd cemetery. Father and I, pushing a box cart up Hermosa Rd, approached the junction with Landscore when the siren sounded. The owner of Gildendale (now Trevimider) was standing in her garden and took mother and grandfather into her house. Before father and I could join them, a plane roared into sight from the direction of Yannon, low enough to see the pilot. Father grabbed me, threw me to the ground beside a high wall and dived on top of me. A machine gun blazed and I heard bullets ricocheting off the road surface. Bombs were dropped nearby so we hurried back to Mulberry St and found our house was undamaged. Soon after starting Brook Hill School, another raid occurred. Bombs fell close by causing many school windows to be blown out. My mother came to meet me along our usual route of Higher Brook St and found it blocked by rubble from bombed houses and broken electricity cables whipping and sparking on top of the high heaps.

We were bombed out of our house by the raid on Sunday 10th January 1943. I was attending Sunday School at the Methodist Church in Somerset Place and mother, who had lost her shoes during the raid, ran down to meet me with no shoes. We hurried back to our badly damaged home. Father was out working on the railway but grandfather was still inside the ruined house. A large dresser in the kitchen had knocked him to the ground but luckily, it came to rest on a chair which took the weight

F.H.A. GUEST HOUSE. ST MARY'S. TEIGNMOUTH. DEVON.

of the dresser and the rubble that followed it down. Grandfather escaped with a slight cut on his head. We moved to Rose Hill Cottage next to West End Garage, opposite Bitton House. The garage being closed, Bill Warren ran his shoe repair business at the front. The cottage and garage belonged to Mr & Mrs Mortimore living at Okehampton and they kindly allowed us to stay in Rose Hill until 1946.

Bomb-damaged roof in Teign St

Pte Thomas Tooley

Born in Plymouth in 1903, Tom came to live in Shaldon, working for ten shillings a week with Mole the Builder. Just 4'10" in height, he was rewarded with £5 for climbing up St Michael's flagpole to untangle the Union Jack for the 1937 Coronation celebrations. Tom joined the Devonshire Regiment and was amongst the many thousands who suffered pneumonia after spending hours in the sea during the evacuation at Dunkirk. Troop ships were crammed so tight that everything other than humans was jettisoned. They were landed near Plymouth and transported very slowly by rail, passing through Teignmouth on their way to Scotland for convalescence. He returned after six months care and joined Teignmouth's ARP. After a few years, Tom contracted TB, followed by cancer and died at the age of 47.

LC Edith Tranckle nee Tooley

Women's Auxiliary Air Force

Edie was born in Albion St, Shaldon in 1925 and was working for Stent the Grocer when she reached the age of 18. Girls had to work in Munitions, the Land Army or join the Forces. She chose to train as a driver with the Women's Auxiliary Air Force. Despite her father's warning never to volunteer, she stepped up when an officer asked if anyone in the company could cook. She was soon catering for the troops and at Stormydown Base near Porthcawl, a tin shed was all that stood between Edie and her cooking range. She won a prize for devising the most economical pudding of triangles of bread and jam, dipped in batter, deep-fried in lard and dusted with sugar. Cooking for British, Canadian, American and Scandinavian pilot officers at Melksham was quite different. The best local produce, beef and fish was put in front

of those young men. It was sad beyond words when so many were killed.

Sidney Tranckle was serving with the Queens Regiment stationed in Teignmouth and married Edie in 1943. She became a Lance Corporal and was twice based at Torquay. As D-Day approached, the road down to the harbour was closed to all traffic except US amphibious vehicles that had travelled overland to rendezvous with those arriving by sea. They were so numerous that it was impossible to see the end of them. In the kitchens of the requisitioned Queens' Hotel, Edie had to get the fire going at 5am each day. She tossed a bit of butter or sugar on the anthracite to speed up the blaze and get the oven hot enough to bake bread rolls. Hundreds of black servicemen from the USA's southern states consumed Edie's food and she still remembers their politeness and mild manner. Unlike our own troops, the Americans had plenty to eat and drink including huge tins of peaches and limitless coffee. After demob in Staffordshire, Edie received a cheque for under £200 for her 1000 days of service. Edie and Sid set up home in Ringmore and raised six children. Edie continued to cater far beyond the needs of her family and ended up as Supervisor Cook at Inverteign School.

Reginald Tribble AB

Reg was born into a family of 5 boys and a girl living in Mulberry St in 1920. He joined the Royal Navy at 20 and on his first night at sea, several men were injured when the ship was attacked just off Flamborough Head near Grimsby. He served on the Earl of Essex, a magnetic minesweeper early on, the majority of his service in the Atlantic on minesweepers and anti-sub ships. His ship was based at Rekyavik where he bumped into another Teignmothian, Ernie "Jockey" Chapman. Dangers lurked in these waters where U-boats took short cuts. His worst experience was a battle with the elements in the Denmark Straits when a 100 mph gale hit their ship. The engines froze up and a kind of anti-freeze had to be put in the gun barrels and ice hacked off the halyards. Reg was denied leave to marry in April 1943 and issued with kit for service in the Far East. His ship was painted in camouflage colours then shortly afterwards, she was called in to Tobermoray and re-painted grey…service in the Far East was off! He renewed and completed his marriage plans one year later than intended. Reg was awarded the 39-45 star, Atlantic star and silver medal for service on a minesweeper and passed them to his son for safekeeping. In the 1960s he was Landlord of Teignmouth's Prince of Wales Inn during its final years before construction of the dual carriageway.

Prince of Wales Inn junction of Fore St & Higher Brook St

Naomi Tucker nee Milford

I was born at Newton Abbot in 1928. My Grandparents Milford lived at 13 Gloucester Rd, where grandfather, a veteran of the Boer and First World War was Caretaker of Teignmouth's Gospel Hall. My sister and I often stayed with them during the summer holidays. One afternoon in 1942 we were invited to see some new kittens at 9 Gloucester Rd. On the way down we saw 2 or 3 planes flying in very low over the Ness. Aunty shouted "It's Gerry!...Run!" As we ran back up the hill, machine gun bullets whistled all around us. We were terrified and ran down into the cellar, reached by stone steps that led off the kitchen. About 10 of us took shelter and suddenly a huge explosion shook the house to its foundations as bombs fell nearby. The sensation of the blast seemed to go right through us and it felt as if the walls closed in and opened out again. Then we were in complete darkness except for the light coming through an airbrick under the front door step. We were unable to get out as the cellar doorway was blocked so Aunty Nan blew her whistle. After sheltering in the back lavatory where pieces of cut newsprint hung from a nail, Grandfather cleared the way to release us. Further down the road where we had been talking to people at their home earlier in the day, there was just a heap of rubble. The family and their home had perished and it was not till years later I discovered that Beryl Hooper nee Smith who was in the same raid attended my school - now Coombeshead College. Number 13 was badly damaged so my Grandparents and aunts who had a shop in The Groves came to live with us for six months then on to other relatives for the next six months. I had nightmares for many years about being shut in but thankfully no longer.

Grandparent Milford's Golden Wedding Anniversary, 13 Gloucester Rd before the 1942 raid

Betty Vickers nee Bace

Above Den Bowling Club in 1949

I was born at Thornley Nursing Home in 1932, the first of three daughters. We were living in Bickford Lane, next to the school when the war began. In September 1942, the boys in the first floor classroom started to shout " Spitfires!" when they spotted four planes coming in over the sea. But these were enemy planes and a few seconds later they machine-gunned the school building. Windows shattered and desks were strewn with flying glass. Plaster from the ceiling fell on us as Miss Reddaway led her class down the stone staircase to the back playground. I would not go into the cellars with the others and ran the few yards across the lane to my Mum and baby sister at home.

Ivy Hindley took a photo of Mum, Pauline and

Mordref Hotel, Eastcliff 1930s with Catholic Church tower visible

me to send to Dad serving with the Devonshire Regiment. I remember taking Pauline in her pushchair to the seafront whilst Mum was at work in Mordref Hotel. A single plane came in from the Ness and riddled the length of the promenade with machine gun fire. Bullets hit the ground sending puffs of concrete up as they ricocheted in all directions. I pulled the hood of the pushchair up hoping to protect Pauline who was waving madly at the pilot! Later on, Mum found a single bullet hole in the hood. Access to the beach was prohibited but after a stretch with no raids, rules were relaxed. I wanted a swim and persuaded Mum to go down on the sands. The tide was out a long way and I had to walk almost the length of the pier to reach the water. Suddenly, four planes came in low over the water, heading straight for town. Mum shouted and screamed for me and we sheltered in under the sun deck. Teignmouth was now defended by anti-aircraft guns that opened fire and the aircraft veered off over the Ness. I remember the day the Yanks came. Everyone was watching on the Den and Mum said I shouldn't go but I went all the same and found wagons full of servicemen as far as the eye could see. They set up a Sick Bay in the Sun Dial Hotel in Den Crescent and built a cookhouse beside the Den Pavilion. At Christmas they gave us a wonderful party with chocolate ice cream and tinned fruit. We went home with sweets and candy bars. They had decorated the Pavilion for the party and when we got home, Mum found white gloss paint all over Pauline's new coat and gave me a good hiding. The Americans' departure was as sudden as their arrival and many of them were killed at Slapton whilst training for the Normandy landings.

For three months, we had no news of Dad whose unit was at the D-Day landings. He had suffered shell shock and lost his bearings. After recuperating in a French hospital, he went out to the Front again. Later, he was flown home on compassionate leave when it was feared that I might lose my leg after being knocked over. I was 13 and recovered well, took up singing and appeared in many local shows. Reflecting on my still-vivid memories of three narrow escapes, it's certain that someone up there was looking after me!

Betty, Pauline and Win Bace

Peter Wale

Peter was a pupil at the Roman Catholic School in Dawlish St. Servicemen sometimes visited the pupils and one day a young man in naval uniform arrived carrying a tiny black cat. The sailor was one of the few who survived the attack on HMS Hood and just after the ship sank, this cat climbed up on his shoulder. He brought the little creature home and his parents cared for it. The school was moved for a while into the church hall further up the hill. The approach was through a doorway in the wall and up a few steps. At about 1.30 one day Peter was returning from lunch break and heard the sound of an aircraft. He took no notice until it flew directly overhead only just above the rooftops. The pilot waved and saluted Peter, who waved back. After the plane moved further away, he saw crosses on the wings and a swastika on its tail and guessed it was surveying the area. The anti-aircraft guns at the seafront opened up but he never discovered if the plane was hit.

As Peter lay in bed in his grandmother's Bitton Avenue home, he heard the high-pitched whistle of a bomb. A long time seemed to pass before it exploded just below in Alexandra Terrace. Like a magic carpet, Peter's eiderdown rose smoothly into the air until it was about one foot high before floating gently down to the bed. He found this a frightening experience. In the road by the Quay, Peter saw hundreds of empty cartridge cases, ejected from machine guns carried by boats berthed by the quay. He also found a small khaki coloured tin with the German eagle embossed on its lid. It was about the size of a matchbox and contained some small bottles of liquid. It had obviously fallen out of an enemy plane and Peter's father, uncertain of their contents, disposed of the bottles.

Overview of Regent St and Triangle 1944

Ruth Westlake

VAD nurse at Exeter Military Convalescent Home

Until the Talkies came in, Ruth played piano for films at Teignmouth's Riviera Cinema and was a great friend of local photographer Ivy Hindley. A gifted singer, she worked with Fleet Photoplays, a film production company based in Torquay. In the 1930s she became known as Madam Ruth Westlake "Devon's Golden Voiced Soprano" singing at various high class venues such as Deller's in Exeter. She sometimes worked with Harry Punchard, a ventriloquist/conjuror and could earn £2 for an evening show whilst her husband collected only ten shillings a week on the dole during the Depression. They scraped together enough money to build a bungalow named Nirvana in Salcombe Dip. She served as a VAD nurse and Geoff, her son remembers that when the sun shone and Ruth was happy, she rushed into the front room to sit at the piano to play and sing songs such as "Some day my Prince will come".

Geoff Westlake

Playing drums (aged 16) with Max Farman Band London Hotel Ballroom 1946

I was born at Exeter in 1931. The evening of Sunday 7th July 1940 was sunny and balmy and my sister Aline and I were on the lawn of our home Nirvana. A twin-engine aircraft appeared from the Newton Abbot direction and travelled at an unhurried pace towards Teignmouth. Two black objects fell from it and my sister and her boyfriend cycled madly into town to find out what had happened. They returned with the news that the pier had been hit during Teignmouth's first raid. Among the casualties was my school friend Reg Barnes who suffered a broken leg when a gaming machine fell on him. I was sent to stay with my grandmother in Milton Abbot but returned home after father had a bad accident when his bicycle was in collision with an army lorry at Broadmeadow. He was bed ridden and eventually it was decided that I was being neglected so I was sent to stay with my aunt in Exeter. Out of the frying pan into the fire! I lived through the most frightening experience of my life...the Exeter blitz with two hours of constant bombing.

I travelled home to see the damage caused by the raid on Salcombe Dip on 5th July 1941. On the night of the raid, my father was asleep with the bedroom window open. One of a stick of six bombs dropped so close that his bed was covered in earth thrown up by the explosion. On our lawn lay a large portion of the bomb's nose cone with its large fins, more or less intact, painted green with a yellow stripe. The pieces ended up in Roberts' scrap yard across the road. My father was repairing an old motorbike in the yard when an aircraft roared from nowhere at about 50 feet and dropped a bomb that travelled almost horizontally. It just missed the railway track, landed about five yards from father then bounced before exploding in a field at Headway Cross about half a mile away. An ME 109 was put on view near the lifeboat station. It cost 3d to enter the roped-off enclosure and sit in the cockpit which, even as a child, I thought quite small. The aircraft seemed to be intact and gave off a chemical smell. I pinched a tiny piece of fabric. It started to rain heavily and we sheltered under its wings.

My mother Ruth and I set off from the Triangle in Gourd's bus on 13th August 1942. As we were going up Fore St, a shop window suddenly blew out in front of the bus and all hell was let loose. From the back of the bus I saw an aircraft screaming low overhead. There were more explosions and the blast from a bomb came right through the bus, throwing me off the back seat. The impact on my ears was terrible. Meanwhile, the bus kept advancing away from the devastation. Approaching Broadmeadow, we breathed sighs of relief but to our horror, saw the gasometers were on fire and we had to pass right beside them! The driver, Duggie Gourd didn't know whether to abandon the bus or continue past the potentially explosive gasometers. My mother, a VAD nurse was helping a woman who had fainted and shouted, "Drive on Duggie! Drive on!" We alighted outside Nirvana in the calm of Salcombe Dip. Two hours later, my father arrived home covered in dust and related how a property next to the bombed Fire Station had collapsed leaving him surrounded by sparking electric wires and water.

Bombs fell on the spots marked X near Nirvana at Salcombe Dip, home of the Westlakes

Cyril Gordon " Son" Westlake Leading Seaman

Gunner on HMS Hunter
K.I.A. Narvik 10th April 1940

Many Teignmothians served their country during World War Two in the armed forces by land, sea and air. Amongst those who paid the ultimate sacrifice was Cyril Gordon Westlake of 2, Ivy Lane known to all as "Son". He grew up as a West Lawn schoolboy with Fred and Roger Matthews, Roy Nathan, Syd and Stan Hook. In 1936 at the age of 18 years, he joined the Royal Navy with his pal, Dennis Cook. Son trained as a seaman at HMS St Vincent, Gosport and joined the destroyer HMS Active on patrol duties in the Mediterranean during the Spanish civil war. He returned home for his first leave during the summer of 1939. One August afternoon, a telegraph boy rode his red bicycle down Ivy Lane bringing a telegram for immediate recall to Devonport. His father, known to all as Carlo, took it across to the pier where Son and Syd were amusing themselves. Son was to rejoin the destroyer HMS Hunter as leading seaman Gunner, manning a 4.7-inch gun. Seven months later, Syd was delighted when he spotted Son on the stern of the Hunter at Scapa Flow, and shouted out and waved to him. Days later, on March 16th, both men survived a daytime air attack on Scapa. After Germany invaded Norway on 9 April 1940, their troop-carrying destroyers went into Narvik Fjord, deep in the Artic Circle. The next day a flotilla of five British destroyers Hotspur, Havock, Hostile and Hunter with the lead ship Hardy attempted recapture following orders to Captain Warburton-Lee to "proceed to Narvik and use discretion for action". Battle action took place in a snowstorm and tremendous damage was inflicted on enemy war and merchant ships before the British ships were driven back. Son Westlake was mortally injured in action at the gun in X turret of the Hunter which suffered shelling. Following a collision with Hotspur, the Hunter sank midstream of Vesfiord, carrying Son with it. Some of the crew managed to get ashore and make their way to freedom in Sweden.

Son's grave is in the sea and his name is recorded on Teignmouth's war memorial. Every year on November 11th he is remembered together with all those from the town who gave their lives for our freedom.

There is no connection between the Westlakes of Nirvana and the above entry.

Pat Wise

I was born at Alwyns Nursing Home, Barnpark Rd in 1937. We lived at 11A Bickford Lane in a house that is still there. On 17th September 1942, I was just leaving Brook Hill School to cross Bickford Lane for home as planes came over. Despite being told not to run, I raced in to my Mum! She discovered a piece of shrapnel lodged in my back. Father, who worked as an engineer at Morgan Giles shipyard, heard that a bomb had dropped in Higher Brook St and ran all the way across town. Helped by fishmonger Phil Nathan, Dad and I got through the rubble and debris of many houses along Brook St on the way to Northumberland Place. Dr Rosalind Cooper, a tall and imposing lady, took us into a house that I believe belonged to people called Cave, close to where Osmonds Lane cuts across. She put me on their kitchen table, cut out the shrapnel and closed the wound on my shoulder blade with 3 or 4 stitches.

Alwyns Nursing and Convalescent Home, Barnpark Road

Doris Wood nee Robins

Sister of Ernest and Reg Robins, also in this volume, Doris was born in Saxe St in 1923. Their father, who had served in the Navy most of his working life, was called into the RNVR. Leaving his job with Teignmouth Electric Light Company, he went down to Devonport where, at the request of a colleague, he agreed to swap a weekend duty. It cost him his life. The base was blitzed with dreadful loss of life. Doris was away with her friend Ada Williams making parachutes at Heathcott's Tiverton factory. She came back to live at home, look after her mother and work as a Rivetter on MTBs in Morgan Giles shipyard. "There were about 10 girls including Pearl Carr and Peggy Broom, working there under the Forelady, Mrs Woodleigh. The timbers for the MTBs were put in a long round pipe to be steamed. There was a dial to control the temperature and when it reached a certain level, the men ran quickly with the timbers and bent them over a template. The Riveters used to take it in turns to hold the dolly whilst the other one used a punch on the "rose". After that, the copper rivet was cut off and we had to tap it all the way around with a hammer. Then we put calico over the timbers and covered that with linseed oil. Then came a second skin of wood. We worked alongside the men including Roy Mills who fitted the planks and clamped them in place." Doris raised her family in Dorset and the pull of home was strong enough to bring her back to Teignmouth in retirement.

**Standing down parade of Home Guard 17th RA Pln 9th Devon.
The Den, Sunday 3rd December 1944**

Gun emplacement at East Cliff after the war

VICTORY

Now thank we all our God and O Worship the King were the hymns selected to accompany prayers and a lesson from the Book of Psalms. The service closed with three verses of the National Anthem and a Blessing

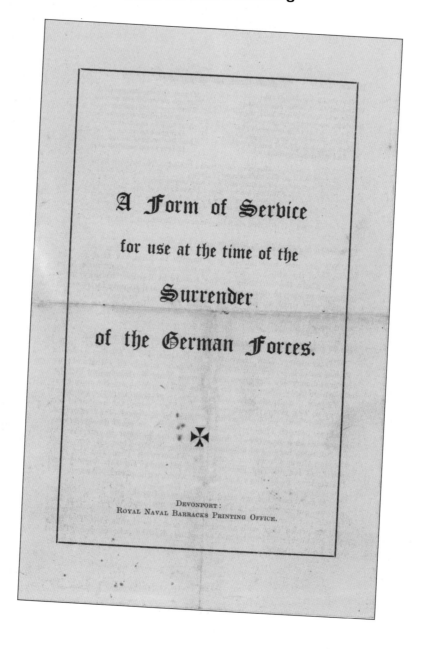

A Form of Service

for use at the time of the

Surrender

of the German Forces.

✠

DEVONPORT:
ROYAL NAVAL BARRACKS PRINTING OFFICE.

VICTORY
Street Parties in May 1945

Kingsdown and Mill Lane

Hutchings Way

VICTORY

Teign View Place

VICTORY

The Groves & Boscowan Place

Tranckle Party

VICTORY

Town Youth Club in front of Den Bandstand

Thanksgiving Service on Shaldon Green

Teignmouth was visited by many frigates and destroyers in the late 1940s when locals delighted in being ferried out for tours aboard.

Wesley(L) and brother Tom Highgate aboard a visiting frigate lying off Teignmouth, late 1940s

HMS Tremadoc Bay at anchor off Teignmouth Pier. Built by Harland Wolf of Belfast, she was launched in March 1945 and visited Teignmouth often. Scrapped in Genoa in 1959

Flooding in Brunswick Street, six weeks before the onset of hostilities

Overcliff Guest House, Dawlish Rd one of many buildings in need of attention after years of military use

Pre-war overview from Breakneck Hill. The fields to the left of Exeter Road (C) were used for military training

Esplanade, winter 1947

The prediction of weather and the ability to forecast accurately was a significant and positive development of the war years. Forecast rooms were established in meteorological stations where information was gathered and interpreted. Radar was used to track storms and small balloons equipped with wireless sent signals back to earth from the upper atmosphere. In the late 40s, as regular trans-Atlantic flights got underway, the need for accurate predictions was even greater. In 1947, a number of ocean weather ships were set up to act as meteorological observatories in the north Atlantic.

Ironically, in this same year, Britain experienced its worst winter in living memory. Food shortages and rationing were still part of post-war daily life but early in the year, a water main failed and local inhabitants were plunged into another domestic crisis. The main supply to Teignmouth ceased after the pipe burst and for six weeks, people managed as best they could. Peggy and Ray Thompson and their small son Terry lived at 4 Bitton St and drew water from a well at Foy's Dairy in Exeter Rd (now Exeter St) holding their supply in a zinc bath. Snow upon snow blanketed the town and from the front bedroom window overlooking St James churchyard, the family watched daily as the level climbed higher and higher against the church wall. It attained a point somewhere between 3 and 4 feet according to their memory of the unforgettable winter of 1947.

BRITAIN DELIVERS THE GOODS

THANKS TO THE BRITISH NAVY

Haldon Aerodrome

The military significance of the Aerodrome created on Little Haldon in the late 1920s by William Parkhouse MBE was included in pages 42 to 44 of Teignmouth at War 1. There is very little evidence of it to be found on the ground in modern times. In October 2002, Teignmouth & Shaldon Museum erected a memorial stone and plaque acknowledging the Aerodrome's foundation and short existence.

Arthur & Joyce Morgan in memorial chapel St Michael's Church 2002

During the 1990s when Arthur was a Churchwarden, he researched the names of all Teignmouth-born civilians and servicemen and women killed by enemy action during the 1939-45 war. The details are recorded in a special volume of memorial.

Facsimile copy of original records

ATTACKS ON TEIGNMOUTH DISTRICT

Date	Place	Time	Casualties Killed.	Wounded.
7.7.1940	Seafront	18.55	1.	20
8.7.1940	Seafront	14.19	Nil	Nil.
21.10.1940	Lindridge	22.45	Nil	Nil
12.12.1940	Wood	22.40	Nil	Nil
15.2.1941	Kingmore District	19.55	Nil	Nil
2.3.1941	Mill Lane, Avenues.	20.03	5	7
8.5.1941	Hospital, Mill Lane	02.15	11	4
15.5.1941	Pier in Sea	05.49	Nil	Nil.
11.6.1941	Rly Line, Holehead Tunnel	19.13	Nil	Nil
5.7.1941.	Salcombe Area	02.40	Nil	Nil.
24.10.1941	Exeter Road	21.15	2	5
7.3.1942	Machine Gunning in Sea off Pier	09.35	Nil	Nil
16.4.1942	Machine Gunning river Teign, Bridge and Ferry, and Fishing boats	20.05 (Alert 20.15)	Nil	Nil
23.4.1942	H.E.Bombs in Sea off Labrador 4.H.E. Bombs on Headway Cross Water main damaged.	(Alert 22.45) 23.15)	Nil	Nil
2.7.1942	H.E.Bombs -junction of Bitton	(Alert		
31.7.42	One H.E.Bomb. Bitton Avenue One H.E.Bombs at the corner of Belgrave Terrace and the Heywoods	19.13 (Alert 19.15)	8	13
13.8.42	8 H.E. bombs (including one UXB) dropped in Teignmouth	17.32 (Alert 17.34)	14	23
2.9.1942	4 H.E.Bombs dropped on Esplanade, Alwyns and Higher Brook Street	15.55 (Alert 15.55)	8	31
3.11.1942	Four H.E.Bombs dropped, two in Teignmouth, two in Salcombe area, District Cannon fired	12.45 Coastal Alert 12.47 F.C. warning 12.50	6	4
10.1.1943	5 H.E.Bombs down on Powderham Terrace and Central Teignmouth	14.30 hrd C.A.Siren 14.30 F.C.Alert 14.38	20	26
18.5.1943	Bitton Park, Teignmouth and Shaldon, Teign House Hotel 2 HE's and over 200 Incendiary Bombs.	02.45 (Alert 02.27)	Nil	Nil
29.5.1944.	Bishopsteignton - Little Haldon Road, 300 yds west of Gipsy Corner and vicinity 1 - 500 KG 6 - 50 K.G 1 - 1200 KG. UXB	01.40 (Alert 01.25)	Nil	Nil.

79   151

2²

Facsimile copy of original records

AIR RAIDS ON TEIGNMOUTH
LIST OF CASUALTIES.

NAME	SEX	APPROXIMATE AGE	ADDRESS	KILLED OR INJURED	RAID
MEDLAND, Joyce	F	16 yrs.	48, Parson St., Teignmouth.	K. S.I. (died from injuries)	7th July, 1940. In sea off Teignmouth Pier.
MATTHEWS, James,	C	14	2, The Strand, "	S.I.	"
BARNES, Reggie	C	9	3, Stanley St. "	S.I.	"
GARRARD, Jina	C	14	61, Second Avenue, "	S.I.	"
VICKERY, Tony	C	12	47, Teign Street, "	S.I.	"
CANN, Betty	C	14	3, New Quay St. "	L.I.	"
BUTLER, Margaret	F	30	44, Fore St. Shaldon.	L.I.	"
TIBBS, Emily	F	59	22, Bickfords Lane, Teignmouth.	L.I.	"
MORTIMORE, Teresa	C	13	21a, Parson St. "	L.I.	"
WILLIAMS, Mrs.	F	77	5, Daimonds Lane, "	L.I.	"
HANCOCK, Sylvia	C	13	64, Second Avenue, "	L.I.	"
MARTIN, Mrs.	F	51	45, Crossley Moor, Kingsteignton.	L.I.	"
RODWELL, R.J.	M	15	13, Coombe Vale, Teignmouth.	L.I.	"

Facsimile copy of original records

NAME	SEX	APPROXIMATE AGE	ADDRESS	KILLED OR INJURED	RAID
HOOK, Leslie George	M	29	Seaman, Royal Navy. 47, Second Avenue, Teignmouth.	K	2nd March, 1941. 5 H.E.Bombs, Mill Lane, & Avenues.
HOOK, Dorcas Irene	F	29	" " "	K	"
HOOK, Delphin Mary	C	3	" " "	K	"
FIELD, Frank	M	54	47, Second Avenue, Teignmouth.	K	2nd March, 1941. (contd)
FIELD, Elsie Jane	F	53	" " "	K	"
CORPS, Gordon	C	11	"Lynfield", Kingsdown, "	L.I.	"
SMITH, Mary	F	69	" " "	L.I.	"
BARNES, Ethel	F	49	45, Second Avenue, "	L.I.	"
BARNES, Elizabeth	F	75	" " "	L.I.	"
PHARE, Evelyn	F	34	49, " "	L.I.	"
PHARE, Sheila	C	14	" " "	L.I.	"
HERBERT, Jane Elizabeth	F	66	"Heswall", Kingsdown, "	K	8th May, 1941. (10 H.E.Bombs, Hospital and Kingsdown,Mill Lane)
WITHEORROW, Rosa	F	56	5, Dagmar St. Shaldon.	K	"
MILNER, Beatrice	F	49	"Lareys", Dawlish Rd. Teignmouth.	K	"
MUNDY, Bessie	F	55	"Coombe Bank",Landscore Rd. "	K	"
COTMORE, Mary Louise	F	60	2, Foresters Terrace, "	K	"
TATCHELL, John Francis	M	80	"Claremont", Bishopsteignton.	K	"
MOORE, Eliza	F	75	"Fairlight", Paradise Rd.Teignmouth.	K	"
ESWORTHY, Rosina	F	69	31, Brunswick St. "	K	"

Facsimile copy of original records

NAME	SEX	APPROXIMATE AGE	ADDRESS	KILLED OR INJURED	RAID
JAMES, Beatrice (Nurse)	F	17	Alberta Mansions, Teignmouth.	K	8th May, 1941 (contd)
TAYLOR, Muriel (Nurse)	F	22	52, Gentwood Rd, Hayton,Nr.Liverpool.	K	do.
BRUNS, Olgar (Nurse)	F	26	"Formosa", Torpark Rd, Torquay.	K	do.
BEARHAM, Percy	C	10	20, Hutchings Way, Teignmouth.	L.I.	do.
STEVENS, Carliss	C	6	23, Daimonds Lane, do.	L.I.	do.
SULLIVAN, M. (Private)	M	19	C.Coy, 70th Batt. Queens Royal Rifles. L.I.	do.	
HERBERT, Henry Edward	M	60	"Heswall", Kingsdown Estate,Teignmouth.	I.	do.

* The following are from Hospital Records as being treated in Hospital, but were not officially reported to A.R.P.

NAME	SEX	APPROXIMATE AGE	ADDRESS	KILLED OR INJURED	RAID
* TURTAN, Rev. B.	M			Shock, cuts & bruises.	do.
* PRIVE, Mrs.	F			do.	do.
* HATHAWAY, Mrs. M.	F			Shock	do.
* PICKE, Mrs.	F			do.	do.
BELLAMY, R.	M	84	"Cathays", Yannon Drive, Teignmouth.	L.I.	2 H.E. Bombs, Exeter Road, 24th October, 1941.
BELLAMY, Kathleen	F	32	do.	L.I.	do.
BELLAMY, Albert	M	34	do.	L.I.	do.
ROFF, George William	M	82	do.	L.I.	do.
EVEL, THOMAS EDRE D	M	45	Mount Everest, Exeter Road, "	K	do.
SHACKELL, GEORGE	M	19	6102621, 70th Queen's Regt. Haldon Military Camp.	K	do.
BOTLEY, Pte. L.J.	M		6103863, do. and 38, Warren Road, Addiscombe, Croydon.	L.I.	do.

144

Facsimile copy of original records

NAME	SEX	APPROXIMATE AGE	ADDRESS	KILLED OR INJURED	RAID
TAYLOR, Percival Palmer	M		26, Gipsy Lane, Hunton Bridge, Watford, & 2, Gloucester Road.	K.	2nd July, 1942. 3 H.E.Bombs Bitton St. Gloucester Rd. & Westbourne Terrace.
PROUT, Florence	F		1, Gloucester Road, Teignmouth.	K	do.
SMITH, Jack Thomas A.H.	C		2, do. do.	K	do.
SMITH, Dick	M		Seaman Royal Navy, 2 Gloucester Rd.	K	do.
PUCKEY, Fessie	F		1, Gloucester Rd., Teignmouth	S.I. (died in hospital)	do.
SMITH, Richard Stephen	M	2,	do.	L.I.	do.
SMITH, Edith	F	2,	do.	S.I. (died in hospital)	do.
SALTER, Charlotte	F	3,	do.	L.I.	do.
WEISS, Edwin	M		"Dudleigh House", do.	S.I.	do.
TAYLOR, Ethel	F		2, Gloucester Rd. Teignmouth.	L.I.	2nd July 1942
DUNFORD, Walter	M		2, Westbourne Tce. do.	S.I.	do.
NEIASS, Edwin	M		6, Albion Place, do.	S.I.	do.
BINKS, Dora	F		"West Holt", Bitton St. do.	L.I.	do.
TAYLOR, Isabel	F	12	2, Gloucester Rd. do.	L.I.	do.
NEIASS, Charles	M	74	Dudleigh House, do.	L.I.	do.
CHEADLE, Florence	F	68	32, Bitton St. do.	L.I.	do.
HURFORD, Harold	M	33	3, Westbourne Tce. do.	L.I.	do.
HURFORD, Dora	F	23	do. do.	L.I.	do.
MILLS, William	M	47	32, Bitton St. do.	L.I.	do.
MILLS, Roy	M	16	do. do.	L.I.	do.
HEXTER, Frank	M	69	4, Westbourne Tce. do.	L.I.	do.
SMITH, Basil	M	32	32, Bitton St. do.	L.I.	do.

Facsimile copy of original records

Name		Age	Address		Status	Notes
FORD, Ada May	F	59	39, Bitton Ave.	do.	K	31st July, 1942. Two H.E.Bombs on Bitton Avenue, & The Heywoods.
CURTIS, Ida Alice	F	59	37, do.	do.	K	do.
HAMLYN, Daisy Winifred X.	F	39	41, do.	do.	K	do.
HAMLYN, Winifred Irene Sheila	C	13	41	do.	K	do.
HAMLYN, Marjorie Asenath	C	9	41, do.	do.	K	do.
GOVIER, Ellen	F	86	41, do.	do.	K	do.
WHITEMAN, Edith Mary	F	50	37, Bitton Avenue, Teignmouth.		K	31st July, 1942.
WHITEMAN, Arthur	M	52	do.	do.	K	do.
WILLIAMS, Frances	F	80	35, do.	do.	L.I.	do.
WILLIAMS, Mary Ann	F	77	do.	do.	S.I.	do.
FAULKIER, Tony	C	9	1, Devonshire Place,	do.	S.I.	do.
PHARE, Evelyn	F	55	19, Coombe Vale Ave,	do.	S.I.	do.
CURTIS, Harry	M	67	37, Bitton Ave,	do.	S.I.	do.
WHITEMAN, Daphne	F	25	do.	do.	S.I.	do.
GOVIER, Lily Annie	F	80	41, do.	do.	S.I.	do.
GOVIER, Nellie	F	80	do.	do.	F.A.P. to Hospital.	do.
HOLDER, Thomas	M	66	3, The Heywoods, Teignmouth		L.I.	do.
SHARLAND, Joan Winifred	F	13	1, Glendaragh Rd.	do.	L.I.	do.
CHEESEMAN, Ada	F	55	2, The Heywoods,	do.	L.I.	do.
BAKER, Rose Ellen	F	72	1, Belgrave Terrace,	do.	L.I.	do.
CLEYDEN, Sarah	F	68	"Lyddington",Hr.Brimley,	do.	L.I.	do.
DENLEY, Lena	F	27	9, Lr.Brook St.,	do.	L.I.	do.

Facsimile copy of original records

NAME	SEX	APPROXIMATE AGE	ADDRESS	KILLED OR INJURED	PAID
BENETT, Florence Rosina	F	38	4, Albion Place, do.	K	13th August, 1942 8 H.E.Bombs, Albion Place, Park St. Barnpark, etc.
TAPP, Alice Maud,	F	66	7, do.	K	do.
CHAMINGS, Carrie	F	72	1, Barnpark Terrace, do.	K	do.
CLODE, William Wallace	M	52	4, Coombe Rd, Teignmouth.	K	13th August, 1942.
COLES, Thelma	C	6	"Isomer", Hr.Brinley, do.	K	do.
SMITH, Hazel Jacueline	C	5	"Amberley" do. do.	K	do.
HODGE, Florence	F	53	2, Myrtle Hill, do.	K	do.
HODGE, Rose	F	51	18, Quarry Park Rd, Peverell, Plymouth.	K	do.
LEE, Alice Jane	F	66	5, Parson Street, Teignmouth.	K	do.
LOOSEMORE, Fredk.John	M	76	52A, Parson St. do.	K	do.
LOOSEMORE, Mary Maria	F	72	do. do.	K	do.
PERROW, Edward John Cook	M	63	54 do.	K	do.
COX, Eliza	F	80	9, Parson Place do.	K	do.
MORTIMORE, Maurice Louis Charles	M	26	"Sunnycrest", Bitton Hill, do.	K	do.
TAPPER, Olive Maude Pasco	F	50	53, Parson St. do.	S.I.	do.
BOYNE, Elizabeth	F	74	6, Parson Place, do.	S.I.	do.
LOCK, Thomas Francis	M	71	6 do. do.	S.I.	do.
ERICKSON, Frederick	M	41	5 do. do.	S.I.	do.
COX, Eli zabeth Ann	F	44	9 do. do.	S.I.	do.
NEIASS, Annie Maria	F	64	6, Albion Place do.	S.I.	do.
STACEY, Lily	F	45	3, Myrtle Hill, do.	S.I.	do.
EVANS, Ruth	F	72	do. do.	S.I.	do.

147

Facsimile copy of original records

NAME	SEX	APPROXIMATE AGE	ADDRESS	KILLED OR INJURED	RAID
					13th August,1942 (contd)
BACE, GEORGE	M	39	4, Grove Avenue, Teignmouth.	S.I.	do.
HOOPER, Janet	C	2½	1a, Barnpark Terrace, do.	S.I.	do.
HOOPER, Emma	F	29	do.	Ll.I.	do.
MOORE, Robert	M	12	do.	L.I.	do.
HATHWAY, Marjorie	F	38	Larksland, Salty Lane, Shaldon.	L.I.	do.
PRINCE, Kitty	F	3 5	3, Brimley Terrace, Teignmouth.	L.I.	do.
GIBBS, William	C	15	3, Myrtle Hill, do.	L.I.	do.
GIBBS, Henry William	M	49	do.	L.I.	do.
HODGE, William	M	50	2, do.	L.I.	do.
WHITCHER, Clara	F	79	2, Parson Street, do.	L.I.	do.
STEPHENS, Edith Elizabeth	F	44	11, do.	L.I.	do.
MITCHELL, Seth	M	77	28, Brunswick Street, do.	L.I.	do.
WATSON, Elizabeth	F	60	"Glenside", Shaldon.	L.I.	do.
PENWILL, Doreen	F	16	"Woodlands Cott: Lr.Brimley,Teignmouth.	L.I.	do.
BULLEY, Mrs,	F	59	17, Wellington Road, Exeter.	L.I.	do.
BLACKMORE, Stella	F	35	13, Lower Brimley, Teignmouth.	L.I.	do.
MINEAR, Louie	F	43	Teignmouth House, Teign St. do.	L.I.	do.
HUMPHRIES, Winnie	F	28	39, Saxe St. do.	L.I.	do.
DAPT, Percy	M	58	4, Lower Brook St. do.	L.I.	do.

Facsimile copy of original records

NAME	SEX	APPROXIMATE AGE	ADDRESS	KILLED OR INJURED	RAID
CORMODE, George	M	51	"Fairlight", Paradise Rd, Teignmouth.	L.I.	13th August,1942. (cont'd)
FRIEND, Winnie	F	25	29, Mulberry St.,	L.I.	do.
LAWREY, William	C	13	40, Willow St.	L.I.	do.
MITCHELL, William	M	40	40, Brunswick St.	L.I.	do.
THOMPSON, Constance	F	59	White Hart Hotel,	L.I.	do.
PRICE, Winnie	F	58	do.	L.I.	do.
WARNE, Donald	C	9	"Cyprus", Thornley Drive,	L.I.	do.
WARNE, Eva	F	19	do.	L.I.	do.
HARRIS, Howard	M	56	4, Wellington St.	L.I.	do.
BOYNE, Rosina	F	24	5, Featherstone Place,	L.I.	do.
BUTCHER, William	M	66	4, do.	L.I.	do.
BUTCHER, Emma	F	58	do.	L.I.	do.
HAYWARD, Bertha	F	60	3, do.	L.I.	do.
HAYWARD, Tercia	F	17	do.	L.I.	do.
CANN, Kitty	F	29	5, Albion Place, Teign St, do.	L.I.	do.
WILLIAMS, Henry John	M	82	11, Hr. Brook Street, do.	K	2nd September,1942. Four H.E. bombs, Esplanade, Alwyns, Hr.Brook St. (2)
WILLIAMS, Elizabeth Mary	F	79	do. do.	K	do.
JAMES, Alice Jemima	F	82	do. do.	K	do.
BE ST, Florence Mary	F	75	10, do. do.	K	do.
BEST, Pauline Voran Brook	F	44	do. do.	K	do.

149

Facsimile copy of original records

NAME	SEX	APPROXIMATE AGE	ADDRESS	KILLED OR INJURED	RAID
GILPIN, Alice Jessie	F	68	St. Rudeaux, Seymour Rd, Newton Abbot.	K	2nd September 1942 (contd)
TURPIN, Rosa Victoria	F	55	Shimpitts, Bishopsteignton.	K	do.
LOOSEMORE, Elizabeth	F	72	8, Landscore Road, Teignmouth.	K	do.
TAYLOR, William	M	33	"Hillside", Bishopsteignton.	S.I.	do.
GRAVENSTEAD, Emma	F	54	Broadlands, Shaldon.	S.I.	do.
SHARLAND, Gwendoline	F	37	"Hurley", Glendaragh Rd, Teignmouth.	L.I.	do.
NORTHWAY, Enid	F	28	Esplanade House, do.	S.I.	do.
HUBBARD, Sheila	C	3½	do.	L.I.	do.
WILLIAMS, George	M	32	Berkeley Hotel, do.	L.I.	do.
BARRETT, Elsie	F		do.	L.I.	do.
BARRETT, John	M		do.	L.I.	do.
CAUSLEY, Alice	F	53	51, Brook Hill, do.	S.I.	do.
FORD, Wilfred Frank	M	43	44, Bitton Avenue, do.	L.I.	do.
TAPP, Lily	F	53	30, Bitton Avenue, do.	L.I.	do.
RENDELL, Frederick	M	41	15, Bitton Road, do.	L.I.	do.
CHAVE, Ivy	F	32	15, Northumberland Place, do.	L.I.	do.
COOK, Lewis Samuel John	M	16	14, Parson Street, do.	L.I.	do.
SMITH, Jessie	F	31	28, Exeter Road, do.	L.I.	do.
LOVERIDGE, Gwen	F	25	15, Coombe Vale Avenue, do.	L.I.	do.
SPEAR, Alfred	M	61	14, First Av., Oakhill, Dawlish	L.I.	do.

Facsimile copy of original records

NAME	SEX	APPROXIMATE AGE	ADDRESS	KILLED OR INJURED	PAID
BEATTY, J.R.		37	29, Hr. Brook St., Teignmouth.	L.I.	2nd September 1942 (cont'd)
SLEEMAN, Alice	F	56	23, do. do.	L.I.	do.
LAURIE, L.		29	26, Brook Hill, do.	L.I.	do.
BLACKMORE, William	M	58	15, Dagmar St., Shaldon.	L.I.	do.
FRAGALL, Fred	M	45	7, Salisbury Terrace, Teignmouth.	L.I.	do.
MOULE, Vera	F	35	6, Saxe Street, do.	L.I.	do.
MILLS, Evelyn	F	20	4, Bickfords Lane, do.	L.I.	do.
BRIDGE, W.		40	17, First Avenue, do.	L.I.	do.
CUTLIFFE, Joan	F	23	Shute Hill Crescent, do.	L.I.	do.
PADDON, Freda	C	9	2, Gladstone Terrace, do.	L.I.	do.
TAPP, Ada	F	36	30, Bitton Avenue, do.	L.I.	do.
SMITH, Fred	M	60	"Arranmore", Buckeridge Rd. do.	L.I.	do.
HAZEL, Cecil	M	57	"Rocklands", Ferndale Rd. do.	L.I.	do.
MEAD, Gladys L.	F		7, Hutchings Way, do.	L.I.	do.
BOORER, Raymond	M	15	15, Park St., do.	K	3rd November, 1942. Four H.E.Bombs, "Gwynfa", Park St. Salcombe area.
BOORER, Rhoda	F	61	do. do.	K	do.
STEVENS, Mary Alexandra	F	29	do. do.	K	do.
STEVENS, Ann Rhoda	F	3 months	do. do.	K	do.
YOUNG, Dora Ellen Powell	F	86	"Gwynfa Nursing Home" do.	K	do.
BOORER, Albert William	M	44	Leading Stoker, Royal Navy, do.	K	do.
GEORGE, Bessie	F	53	13, Park Street, Teignmouth.	L.I.	3rd November, 1942.
SAUNDERS, Mabel	F	45	do. do.	L.I.	do.
PORTER, Eliza	F	96	"Gwynfa Nursing Home" do.	L.I.	do.
TAYLOR, Winifred	F	43	do. do.	L.I.	do.

Facsimile copy of original records

NAME	SEX	APPROXIMATE AGE	ADDRESS		KILLED OR INJURED	RAID
BROOK, Bernard Edward J.	M	27	8, Alexandra Terrace,	do.	K	10th January, 1943. 5 H.E. Bombs,
BROOK, Eileen Martha	F	27	do	do.	K	Powderham Terrace, Alexandra "
BROOK, John Alexander C.	C	20 months	do.	do.	K	& Central Teignmouth.
BROOK, Edward John C.	M	19	do.	do.	K	do.
PRATT, Jessie	F	65	7, do.	do.	K	do.
PRATT, George William	M	30	do.	do.	K	do.
STEPHENS, Charles Francis	M	60	21, Saxe Street,	do.	K	do.
COUSINS, Violet May P.	F	32	16, Chapel Street,	do.	K	do.
HASTINGS, Helena	F	54	4, Powderham Terrace,	do.	K	do.
BRANCHETT, Sidney James	M	50	5, do.	do.	K	do.
CHEVERTON, Agnes Blanche	F	57	5 do.	do.	K	do.
COLEMAN, Samuel John	M	80	do.	do.	K	do.
COLEMAN, Jane Bowen Harris	F	79	do.	do.	K	do.
COLEMAN, Olive Warwick	F	54	do.	do.	K	do.
GODDARD, Florence Wilson	F	72	do.	do.	K	do.
HAMBLEY, Kate Evans	F	82	do.	do.	K	do.

Facsimile copy of original records

NAME	SEX	APPROXIMATE AGE	ADDRESS	KILLED OR INJURED	RAID
RENDELL, William Francis	M	52	5, Powderham Terrace, Teignmouth.	K	10th January, 1943
RENDELL, Peter Francis	M	17	do.	K	do.
SKINNER, Jessie	F	32	4, Hermosa Road,	K	do.
SKINNER, Herbert Lionel *	M	37	do. *P/Mtr Yo.MX.106852 H.M.S.President V" Highgate, London, N.6)	K	do.
COLEMAN, Harold	M	48	5, Powderham Terrace, Teignmouth.	S.I.	do.
RENDELL, Irene	F	50	do.	S.I.	do.
GUPPY, Dennis	C	9	"Fursey Down, HR.Woodway Rd. do.	S.I.	do.
MILLER, Samuel	M	57	4, Hermosa Road,	S.I.	do.
WEBB, Dennis	M	11	47, Coombe Road,	L.I.	do.
WEBB, Richard	M	14	do.	S.I.	do.
COLLINS, Mark	M	68	9, Bitton Street,	L.I.	do.
COLLINS, Ethel	F	63	do.	L.I.	do.
SHIMMEL, Frank	M	54	"Highlands", Yannon Drive,	L.I.	do.
COATES, Frederick William	M	73	11, Alexandra Terrace,	L.I.	do.
SALTER, Alfred	M	77	20, Salisbury Terrace,	L.I.	do.
STOCKER, Barbara	C	14	5, Grove Terrace,	L.I.	do.
STOCKER, Beryl	C	7	do.	L.I.	do.
SPENCE, Ann	F	66	24, Saxe Street,	L.I.	do.

Facsimile copy of original records

NAME	SEX	APPROXIMATE AGE	ADDRESS	KILLED OR INJURED	RAID
BATCOCK, John	C	9	18, Fore Street, Teignmouth.	L.I.	10th January, 1943
RIDDLE, Frank	M	54	1, Coldrey Cottage, do.	L.I.	do.
RIDDLE, Minnie	F	53	do.	L.I.	do.
NEWCOMBE, Eliza	F	80	6, Speranza Grove, do.	L.I.	do.
WOOLWAY, Eliza	F	65	12, Teign Street, do.	L.I.	do.
HELLIER, Ronald	M	23	378, Battery Road, Brixham.	L.I.	do.
LEVESBY, Maurice	M	22	do.	L.I.	do.
HALLETT, Thomas	M	56	19, Saxe Street, Teignmouth.	L.I.	do.
HALLETT, Annie	F	46	do.	L.I.	do.
GEARY, Roy	C	6	39, Teign Street, do.	L.I.	do.
COLBURN, Martha	F	33	11, Alexandra Terrace, do.	L.I.	do.
CASTLE, Michael	C	8	18, Fore Street, do.	L.I.	do.
EVANS, Alice	F	74	30, Parson Street, do.	L.I.	do.

154